SECRET CIA

21 Insane CIA Operations That
You've Probably Never Heard of

BILL O'NEILL

ISBN: 978-1-64845-083-9

DON'T FORGET YOUR
FREE BOOKS

TABLE OF CONTENTS

Introduction 1

Capturing the Hearts and Minds of Americans 4

The Pen Is Mightier Than the Sword 4

The FBI Had Nothing on the CIA's Domestic Spying
Program 10

President Johnson Hated Commies.. 11

We Have Met the Enemy and He Is Us 12

HTLINGUAL.. 14

RESISTANCE.. 15

MERRIMAC.. 15

Nixon and CHAOS... 16

US Government Sanctioned Rape, Torture, and Murder 19

The Provincial Reconnaissance Units 21

The Kind of Stuff You See on Movies 23

The End of an Era?.. 25

John Chambers and the CIA 27

The Real-Life Mission Impossible.. 28

The Real-Life *Argo* 30

Did You Know? **34**

A True False Flag Operation **36**

Castro Has to Go..37

Battleground Miami...39

Sex, Drugs, Rock n' Roll, and the CIA **42**

Not a Trip You'd Want to Take 43

The Show Must Go On...45

Sex and Drugs 47

The Drug Smuggling CIA? Part One **50**

Air America 51

Guns, Drugs, and Death in the Golden Triangle.....................53

Cats Make Great Pets, Not-So-Great Spies..............................**56**

An Eager Operation 57

Operation Kitty Goes Live 59

Did You Know? **61**

So, There Really Was Something to That Anti-Vax Thing in Pakistan...**63**

A CIA Asset? 65

We're Here to Help You...66

The CIA Couldn't Kill Castro...**69**

Operation Mongoose 70

Exploding Cigars, Poison Pens, and TB..................................73

From CIA to Feminist Icon **77**

An Unlikely Asset...78

Spying on the Chinese from the Top of the World **84**

Building the Bomb..85

Things Don't Always Go as Planned 86

A Nuclear Meltdown 91

CIA Blowup Dolls.. **92**

Keeping It Real 92

Defecting with the JIB 96

Did You Know? **99**

The First Earth Battalion, Remote Viewing, and Other CIA Paranormal Experiments **101**

The First Earth Battalion... 102

Remote Viewing and ESP.. 103

Grass Roots Political Movements or CIA Operations? **107**

Revolution Is Fun!.. 109

Moving Closer to the West.. 111

CIA Porn **114**

Sukarno and Sexual Blackmail 115

Saddam Hussein and Osama bin Laden Were Gay? 118

The Gong Show and the CIA... **120**

From TV Producer to Assassin?...................................... 121

Did You Know? **126**

No One Really Cares about Guatemala **128**

The Fruits of Communism 129

A Phony War 131

Exporting CIA Violence South of the Border **135**

Fighting the Red Scourge 136

Not an Airplane Ride You'd Want to Take 139

The Drug Smuggling CIA? Part Two **143**

Funding the Revolution 145

Contras, Cartels, and Cocaine Cowboys 146

If You Think They're Watching You, They Probably Are **150**

First, They Had It, Then It Was Gone 151

Conclusion **155**

INTRODUCTION

Welcome to *Secret CIA: 21 Insane CIA Operations That You've Probably Never Heard of*, the book that peels back some of the most bizarre and sometimes brutal missions of the world's most notorious intelligence agency - or at least, as far as we're allowed to do! Chances are, if you've picked this book up and proceeded this far, you're the kind of person who questions things and doesn't always accept everything at face value.

If so, then this is the book for you.

As the title states, this book is a wild look at some of the craziest, and most intense missions the CIA has done or at least has purported to have done.

Due to the nature of the subject, not all the missions detailed in this book have been acknowledged by the CIA, and a couple has been vociferously denied by the "agency," even in the face of mountains of evidence that says otherwise. But even though we don't have special clearance, we're going to take a look at them anyways!

Some of the operations profiled here can only be described as strange, leading one to wonder how the CIA, which is billed as a collection of smart people, would even think of such things. There was actually an idea to attach listening devices to cats in order to listen in on Soviet spies! Now, if that isn't a little crazy, then I don't know what is.

And despite operating at a time when the United States was much more politically and socially conservative, the CIA seemed to have had a preoccupation with drugs and sex workers during the 1950s and '60s.

You'll read about how they combined the two areas for one particularly outlandish project.

We also profile some interesting characters within the CIA, such as a couple of officers who became known for creating disguises like those in the TV show *Mission Impossible*, which leads to a theme that pops up throughout this book - the connection between Hollywood and the CIA.

Yes, there is a connection.

Among the wackier missions that we'll profile are the interesting and innovative uses that the CIA came up with for blow-up sex dolls. Yes, you read the correctly, blow-up sex dolls!

And then there was game show host Chuck Barris' claim that he was a CIA assassin. As ridiculous as that claim is, once you've read all these other stories, you'll see it may not be so far out of the realm of possibility.

And after reading the rest of this book, you'll also see that the CIA hasn't been above using assassination, torture, beatings, rape, mind control, and a host of other human rights' violations to get what they need.

In addition to 21 stories that will boggle your mind and keep you on the edge of your seat, four "Did You Know?" sections will present five factoids each about the CIA and some of the strangest missions in its history.

So, hang on, strap in, and get ready for a wild ride through 21 of the strangest and most ridiculous operations ever done by the CIA.

CAPTURING THE HEARTS
AND MINDS OF AMERICANS

The Central Intelligence Agency (CIA) is tasked with gathering intelligence on foreign nationals and governments. Whether it is to watch foreign "diplomats" on American soil or to make contact with those who have vital information overseas, the CIA's overarching mission concerns spying, where information is a commodity and sometimes elaborate missions are used to gather information. One of these missions was known as 'Operation Mockingbird'.

Or supposedly known as 'Operation Mockingbird'.

Although it's never been officially acknowledged by the CIA, Operation Mockingbird is believed to have been a very ambitious, yet not too successful plot by the Agency to influence Americans' opinions through media manipulation during the Cold War. Operation Mockingbird was also a way for the CIA to build a vast intelligence network in foreign countries in every corner of the globe.

The Pen Is Mightier Than the Sword

According to American journalist Deborah Davis, and the 1975 US Senate select committee known as the Church committee,

Operation Mockingbird was the brainchild of legendary spook Frank Wisner. Wisner wasn't just some ordinary run-of-the-mill spy; he was actually one of the founders of the CIA who began his career with the CIA's predecessor organization, the Office of Strategic Services (OSS), in 1943.

Wisner helped form the CIA from the OSS after World War II and became its second director in 1951. For the next ten-plus years, until he retired in 1962, Wisner had his hands in many revolutions, insurgencies, and civil wars around the world. He was an ardent anti-communist who believed the ends justified the means, and as he looked at his adversaries in the Soviet Union, he realized that the CIA was playing catch up to the KGB.

The Americans and their NATO allies may have had more nukes and better overall military technology in the 1950s, but the Soviets and their allies were by far the better spies. Whenever a technological advance was made in the West, Eastern Bloc spies quickly stole the ideas for their masters back in Moscow.

Granted, the KGB and other Eastern Bloc intelligence agencies didn't have to deal with civil rights organizations and could basically do as they pleased within their own borders, but as you'll see throughout this book, the CIA rarely allows laws and concepts like freedom, to get in the way of its missions.

Still, the CIA did face restrictions that the KGB just didn't have.

The situation gave Wisner constant consternation, but he eventually saw that Soviet spying methods, as well as their ability to foment revolution and insurgencies, were highly effective, so he decided to use many of those tactics in CIA operations.

When Wisner watched how the KGB and other Eastern Bloc intelligence organizations controlled the press on the other side of the Iron Curtain, as well as many Western far-left publications, he decided to initiate Operation Mockingbird to do the same thing in the West.

According to Davis, Wisner first approached *Washington Post* co-owner Phil Graham about his plan to recruit an army of news editors and journalists to spread anti-communist propaganda at home to Americans as well as to spy on the Soviets and communist sympathizers overseas. Wisner thought Graham, who was born and raised in South Dakota, was predisposed to the ideology of the operation, and most importantly he had extensive contacts in the American media industry.

Wisner was right. Graham enthusiastically joined the operation.

Using information provided by Graham, the CIA began recruiting anywhere from between 50 to 400 journalists to take part in the operation. The CIA appealed to the patriotism of some, offered lucrative rewards to others, and when those didn't work, blackmail was always an option.

It wouldn't be true cloak and dagger without some good, honest blackmail, right?

The truth is that getting the press to write anti-communist articles in the 1950s wasn't too difficult. It was the era of McCarthyism and the Second Red Scare, so no journalists, who tended to be more liberal on the political spectrum, wanted to be seen as supporting communism or the Soviet Union.

But the second, and some would say, most absurd part of Operation Mockingbird - using journalists to gather intelligence - was a little trickier.

The CIA's intelligence-gathering during Operation Mockingbird blurred its original mission of only spying on foreign people and institutions, which many say threatened the very nature of the free press and the First Amendment. The CIA funded many of the operations of the United States National Student Association (NSA), founded in 1947 as an umbrella group of the national student government and organizations. The CIA began funding NSA activities in the 1950s, and according to a 1967 article in the leftist magazine *Ramparts*, the money was used to influence the course of these groups and its members were used as spies and assets.

Another newspaper front the CIA partially ran was the *Rome Daily American*.

The *Rome Daily American* was an English-language newspaper started by American soldiers after World War II ostensibly to provide news for American soldiers stationed in Europe. As with the NSA, the CIA contributed money to the *Rome Daily American*, which allowed it to chart its editorial course as well as place important assets inside the organization.

In addition to funding and influencing journalist organizations and newspapers, the CIA is even said to have funded the 1954 animated film *Animal Farm*, which was based on the George Orwell novel of the same name.

The extent of the CIA's journalist spy network has never been revealed, but it is believed to have been quite vast.

Through Graham, the CIA developed assets at *The New York Times, Newsweek,* and most of the major television news networks. The CIA was then able to post eyes and ears in most countries around the world, including the communist countries of the Eastern Bloc.

According to famous American journalist Carl Bernstein, who is best known for uncovering the Watergate scandal, the CIA used up to 400 journalists for these purposes. He stated that many of these journalists were passive plants of the CIA, merely passing information in conversations but never becoming involved in any in-depth missions.

But some journalists *did* play a more active role in CIA activities.

Some journalists were known to have shared their staff with the CIA and others openly worked with the Agency.

The CIA also had its officers pose as legitimate journalists to gain access to Eastern Bloc countries, where they could gather information, turn sources, and even meet with spies, officers, and contacts behind the Iron Curtain.

Notably, journalists who worked with the CIA ranged on the political spectrum from liberal to conservative - and even included Pulitzer Prize winners!

The CIA's journalist assets were also used to inform on their colleagues, namely those who were thought to be too liberal, as they were seen as potential communist sympathizers or "fellow travelers." The CIA would then put these journalists on a list and monitor them, or they would engage in a smear campaign against them, with the result often being blacklisting and banishment from the industry.

Of course, when all of this was exposed in the 1975 Church Committee and later newspaper articles and books, Americans viewed the revelations with ambivalence. The Cold War was still raging, so most Americans saw any efforts to stem the communist tide as a good thing.

But a few alarms were raised.

Although the CIA denied the existence of Operation Mockingbird, a CIA document declassified in 2007 titled the "Family Jewels" revealed that at least two American journalists were spied on by the Agency in 1963, and as the saying goes, "where there's smoke there's fire." The paper curiously refers to "Project Mockingbird," which was a program initiated by President Kennedy to identify leaks of sensitive information.

For many people, the revelation of *Project* Mockingbird proves that *Operation* Mockingbird was a real operation.

And then there's that famous quote by former CIA director William Casey.

While he was CIA director from 1981 to 1987, he is reported to have said, *"We'll know our disinformation campaign is complete when everything the American people believes is false."*

Some deny that he said that, while others, such as the former assistant to the chief domestic policy advisor to President Ronald Reagan, Barbara Honegger, said they were present when the words were uttered. Those in the latter camp say that the quote is not only proof that Operation Mockingbird was very real but also that it never ended.

THE FBI HAD NOTHING ON THE CIA'S DOMESTIC SPYING PROGRAM

So, we've already seen that although the CIA's mission is to gather intelligence on foreign nationals and governments that may pose a threat to the United States, the missions don't always follow that script. Almost from the time the CIA was founded, the Agency unofficially broadened its program to involve domestic operations, including spying on American citizens.

For the most part, though, spying on and investigating Americans deemed to be a threat to the US government has been the purview of America's equally famous (or infamous) alphabet agency, the FBI.

As the Cold War heated up in the 1950s, and as the CIA was conducting Operation Mockingbird, the FBI started its own ambitious domestic spying program known as the "Counter Intelligence Program" or COINTELPRO.

COINTELPRO ran from 1956 to 1971, during which time hundreds of organizations and groups were investigated. Since it was the Cold War, the FBI primarily focused COINTELPRO on leftist groups, such as the Students for a Democratic Society and the Weather Underground, but also went after ethnic nationalist groups like the Black Panthers, the American Indian Movement, and the Young Lords.

And so as not to discriminate, COINTELPRO also targeted far-right groups such as the Ku Klux Klan and the Minutemen.

So, if you were politically active in the 1960s and not in the Democrat or Republican parties, chances are you and your group had a COINTELPRO file.

The FBI not only investigated radical groups and individuals in COINTELPRO operations but also infiltrated groups and instigated many to commit criminal activity. The FBI's active involvement in criminal activity led to many criminal charges being dropped against COINTELPRO targets, but the FBI and its director J. Edgar Hoover didn't seem to mind; COINTELPRO was meant to discredit its targets as much as it was intended to lead to arrests.

By the late 1960s, those in the American intelligence community saw COINTELPRO as a big success and something they could emulate. The CIA had plenty of ideas and resources to put its own operation into effect that would make COINTELPRO look like child's play.

President Johnson Hated Commies

When Lyndon B. Johnson became President of the United States in 1963 after President Kennedy was assassinated, most people didn't know much about the former senator from Texas, or what to expect. As it turned out, love or hate him, Johnson proved to be like no previous president. The Southern Democrat often went against the segregationist wing of his party on racial issues and was a big advocate for expanding the federal government's influence and power through programs such as Medicare and Medicaid.

But Johnson was also an ardent anti-communist.

In fact, Johnson pretty much led the wave of politicians during that era who were liberal on many domestic issues but very conservative when it came to communism. Johnson was the president who sent the most troops to Vietnam, which he said was to contain communism, and he took a tough stance against the Soviet Union and communist China in other conflicts around the world.

Johnson also took a tough stance against communists in the USA.

As Johnson believed in the benefits of a bigger federal government, he saw the government as a tool to fight communism at home. Although COINTELPRO was going strong during Johnson's term and a half in office, the tough-talking Texan wanted to do more. So, in 1967, he tasked the CIA with devising its own operation to spy on American dissidents. The operation was carried out through the CIA branch known as the Domestic Operations Division, which as the name denotes was designed to work primarily on American soil.

Operation CHAOS was born.

We Have Met the Enemy and He Is Us

Once Operation CHAOS was initiated, the CIA wasted little time, or resources, making it the largest domestic spying program in American history. More than 7,200 Americans were targeted and had files created for them. While many of these people were radicals, some were merely casual acquaintances of those who were and others were just those interested in politics who attended a demonstration, received political literature in the mail or had even made controversial comments at a university.

Operation CHAOS was also quite organized, with most of its files being saved in a computer index. A total of 300,000 civilians had their names mentioned in these files and more than 1,000 organizations from across the political spectrum were monitored, although as with COINTELPRO, most of those investigated were on the left wing.

After all, Johnson was anti-communist and as much as he may have supported the Civil Rights Movement, he believed that it was vital to separate any possible communist connection to the movement or any of his domestic government policies.

So, much like Operation Mockingbird, Operation CHAOS became a program whereby Americans were targeted in ways that were usually unethical and often illegal. And as far as funding was concerned, the sky was the limit for Operation CHAOS. It's estimated that Operation CHAOS went more than 500% over its budget for domestic operations.

But when you're the CIA, budgets really don't mean anything.

With an astronomical budget and authorization from the President, the CIA had plenty of tools and officers to carry out CHAOS, which was divided into three primary sub-projects: HTLINGUAL, MERRIMAC, and RESISTANCE.

HTLINGUAL

HTLINGUAL began as a separate operation in 1953 - before Operation CHAOS went into effect to monitor mail coming and going from the United States and the Soviet Union and other communist nations. Remember, this was the '50s, so when we're talking mail, we mean snail mail (the kind that you actually *write* in a letter, put in an envelope, and mail), not email, so it took plenty of officers and man-hours to carry that out.

The extent of HTLINGUAL has never been revealed, although the CIA has admitted to its existence.

Before HTLINGUAL was incorporated into Operation CHAOS, only the names and addresses on the envelopes were recorded, but after the operation went into effect, many letters were opened and read. Notable activists like Martin Luther King Junior, politicians such as Senator Hubert Humphrey, and chess grandmaster Bobby Fisher were among the more famous Americans who had their snail mail correspondences to and from the Eastern Bloc investigated.

The reality is, though, that many Americans caught up in HTLINGUAL were just ordinary people sending mail to and from family and friends caught behind the Iron Curtain. Ironically, most of these people expected the KGB and other Eastern Bloc intelligence agencies to read their mail, but they probably didn't think the same thing was happening in the good ole U S of A!

As the late 1960s rolled around, things got pretty wild on American college campuses. Student activist groups of that era ranged from being conscientious objectors to the Vietnam War to radical Marxists/communists like the Students for a Democratic

Society. To the CIA, though, they were all peas in the same pod that needed to be smashed.

Enter Project RESISTANCE.

RESISTANCE

Project RESISTANCE was the second major sub-operation of Operation CHAOS, focusing on recruiting friendly informants on college campuses. The assets of Project RESISTANCE tended to be politically conservative professors and other university staff, such as security guards and maintenance workers, who reported the left-wing political activity to their handlers. It's estimated that from 1967 to 1973, more than 12,000 college students and professors were put under surveillance in Project RESISTANCE.

The relative success of Project RESISTANCE opened the door for the CIA to initiate an even bolder sub-op on America's college campuses—Operation MERRIMAC.

MERRIMAC

With the information gleaned from Project RESISTANCE, the CIA placed its own officers in several students and leftist groups in Operation MERRIMAC to gather more information and render some of these groups ineffective. And since the CIA wasn't really supposed to be monitoring American citizens on American soil in the first place, they apparently dispensed with any pretenses of doing things legally.

Project MERRIMAC officers routinely broke into their targets' homes and tapped their phone lines without warrants. False flag operations, such as starting violence at political demonstrations, was also an alleged tactic of CIA officers. The CIA really didn't care about the legality of what they were doing because they aren't a law enforcement organization and they generally disavowed knowledge of their operations anyway.

Besides, they're the CIA, so they can do anything, right? Or at least that's what some in the Agency believed.

But the reality is that things had become pretty confusing by 1968. With Operation CHAOS in full swing, its officers often unknowingly rubbed shoulders with COINTELPRO officers and assets, or undercover officers from local, county, and state police agencies. Some of these organizations were so thoroughly infiltrated by law enforcement and alphabet agencies that most of their members were CIA, FBI, or police informants.

And when Richard Nixon entered the White House in 1969, the scope of Operation CHAOS only increased.

Nixon and CHAOS

Nixon was the opposite of Johnson in many ways, but they were both ardent anti-communists, so when the former took the oath of President, he continued and even expanded Operation CHAOS.

Under Nixon, the CIA and FBI were brought closer regarding domestic surveillance with the creation of the International Committee on Intelligence (ICI), which was chaired by FBI director J. Edgar Hoover. Nixon had 50 Operation CHAOS officers at his disposal, many of whom worked for years undercover with radical groups to establish their revolutionary street cred.

By 1970, President Nixon had the largest domestic spying apparatus at his fingertips, but things, and the times, were quickly changing.

The first major blow to Operation CHAOS's activities was when the FBI shut down COINTELPRO in 1971. Although the FBI continued - and still does by their own admission - to investigate and infiltrate political groups on both ends of the political spectrum, the official end of the program meant that the CIA lost an important resource. Operation CHAOS also lost part of its reason for existing, as the intelligence it gathered was often funneled to COINTELPRO operatives.

The next major blow came when the Watergate scandal came down on Nixon and his administration. The scandal not only pushed Nixon out of office, but it also exposed the many shenanigans he and his supporters did to keep him in office, among which was the misuse of American intelligence agencies.

The final blow was the changing times.

By the mid-1970s, the counter-culture scene was all but over. The Vietnam War had ended, racial segregation was done, and the campus radicals of the '60s had either moved on to become professors or sold out and joined corporate America. Most Americans were quite willing to leave the late 1960s and early 1970s behind, but they were also open to peeling back the sheets and looking at some of the nefarious activities everyone engaged in during that period.

In 1974, journalist Seymour Hersh exposed Operation CHAOS, reporting that it had been shut down in 1973 during the Watergate scandal. A congressional investigation of Operation

CHAOS was done in 1975, where the CIA actually admitted to the operation but claimed it was closed.

Many were happy to hear that the CIA had seemingly learned the error of its ways, but others who are more skeptical, point to CIA involvement in the 2016 presidential election as proof that the ghosts of Operation CHAOS still haunt the US.

US GOVERNMENT SANCTIONED RAPE, TORTURE, AND MURDER

The Vietnam War is considered by historians to have lasted from 1955 to 1975, but those dates, much like the war itself, are a little murky. Since the US never officially declared war on North Vietnam, it's difficult to say exactly when American involvement transitioned from "advisors on the ground" to full-scale military operations. Therefore, typically, the period from the first American involvement with advisors to the fall of Saigon in 1975 to communist forces is used to mark the length of the war.

For the most part, though, American involvement in Vietnam was heaviest from the mid-1960s until 1972 when President Nixon began his second term and started negotiations with North Vietnam.

So, the Vietnam War was not a conventional war in the sense that American involvement wasn't clearly defined at the time, but it was also an unconventional war in many ways on the ground.

Although North Vietnam had a conventional army that was well-funded and supplied by the Soviet Union, and it did engage in some major battles against the American, South Vietnamese, and Australian and New Zealand forces (yes, the Aussies & Kiwis were in Vietnam), most American military activities took place in South Vietnam, far from the North Vietnamese forces.

The American military mission was to support the South Vietnamese Army and government in its fight against the communist insurgency movement known as the Viet Cong (VC).

But how does a standard, conventional military, such as the American armed forces were in the 1960s, fight an unconventional war? Well, you have to gather intelligence about your enemy, you have to think like your enemy, and it doesn't hurt to fight dirty.

So, in 1965, as American involvement in Vietnam was escalating from small groups of advisors to full combat battalions, the government realized it had to use different tactics to fight the VC. The Army's Special Forces Battalion, known as the "Green Berets," had by that time already been involved in countless missions in the South Vietnamese interior. They served as the first military advisors to the South Vietnamese Army and also did some rudimentary intelligence gathering.

But as effective as the Green Berets were in training the South Vietnamese, their intelligence gathering was inadequate.

So, the government decided to call in the experts.

The CIA was given free rein in Vietnam to do what it does best, gather intelligence - this time on the VC. The Phoenix Program was the codename of the CIA's intelligence-gathering mission in Vietnam, which included plenty of kidnappings, torture, and assassinations, from 1965 through 1972. The CIA pointed out that Phoenix Program was quite successful, as it helped to reveal unknown VC leaders and cells, plus helped give the South Vietnamese forces an advantage for a limited time.

But critics of the operation ask, were the tactical advantage of the Phoenix Program worth the loss of humanity that came with it?

The Provincial Reconnaissance Units

CIA officer Peer de Silva was given the dubious task of running the Phoenix Program from Saigon, the capital of South Vietnam. Although his name may not sound very intimidating, Silva was the kind of person who was born to be a spook. He graduated from the United States Military Academy at West Point in 1941 and immediately entered the Army as an officer. Silva may not have graduated at the top of his West Point class - actually, he graduated near the bottom - but he possessed those intangible skills that made him successful in intelligence.

Nerds can make good spies, but they're usually nerds with a touch of badass and a moral compass that is lacking.

Silva's first major gig was in counterintelligence for the Manhattan Project, and after that, he moved on to work with the CIA's forerunner, the OSS. After the war, Silva joined the CIA, learned Russian, and did several operations in Europe where he successfully turned and used informants and assets behind the Iron Curtain.

Silva also had his hand in revolutions and coups in Hungary and South Korea.

So, Silva was the perfect guy to lead the Phoenix Program: he was a veteran intelligence officer, loyal to the cause, and knew how to turn assets.

The first step in the Phoenix Program was to establish secret interrogation centers throughout South Vietnam. These centers could be anything from a building rented in a city to a shed in the middle of the jungle. The important thing was for them to be somewhat isolated so that people wouldn't hear the screams coming from them.

The next important part of the Phoenix Program was getting people to do the dirty work for them. CIA officers built their own networks of assets and informants throughout South Vietnam, but even the officers who spoke Vietnamese could only get so far, so they needed the Vietnamese to do most of the "fieldwork."

Much of the task was handed to the Provincial Reconnaissance Units (PRUs), which were South Vietnamese paramilitary units comprised of former and current police officers, former military, and others who had an axe to grind with the communists, such as Catholics, businessmen, and anti-communists.

The PRUs gathered evidence of VC networks from local sources, which included former VC members, and gave the information to the CIA. Then, CIA officers would sift through the information and determine what was real and needed to be followed up on and what was disinformation intended to get someone in trouble for personal reasons.

Theoretically, for a PRU unit to arrest someone for being involved with the VC, three separate pieces of evidence were needed, although what constituted evidence often depended on the PRU units in the field or the CIA officer in charge.

PRU units would sometimes accompany American or South Vietnamese military units into villages determined "hot zones," but they usually carried out missions alone. A typical PRU mission involved units entering a village with plenty of noise and guns brandished, and then all suspects being rounded up and brought to a nearby CIA center.

Then the real crazy stuff began.

The Kind of Stuff You See on Movies

During the 1980s, there was a seemingly endless production of Vietnam movies. The reason behind the Vietnam popularity of that decade had a lot to do with collective guilt over how returning American servicemen and women were treated, plus the general conservatism of the '80s. Some of the films were set during the war, while others were more ambitious, featuring action stars of the era such as Chuck Norris going back to "Nam" to rescue American POWs.

One thing all those movies had in common was the depiction of the North Vietnamese/communists as an exceptionally cruel enemy.

In these movies, Americans often found themselves facing such cruel and unusual forms of torture as being held in small cages and starved, multiple beatings with any number of objects, and the use of snakes and other animals to elicit responses.

As much as the North Vietnamese and the VC did, in fact, use various forms of torture, the CIA became the master of using torture during the Phoenix Program.

Once the PRUs brought suspected VC members to a CIA center, the torture began almost immediately.

The torture ran the gamut, from run-of-the-mill beatings and rapes to more elaborate types of violence.

If the suspect confessed after an initial beating, he or she would then be pressed for specific information about VC weapons caches, the cell structure and numbers of the VC in the area, and names and locations of VC leaders. If the target/suspect was deemed to have adequately cooperated, then the CIA could consider the target "neutralized." The target would then return to his or her village and would more than likely continue to work as a secret asset for the PRUs and the CIA.

Of course, not every VC member "neutralized" was let off with a simple beating. The VC had plenty of support in the countryside and many were ardent believers in the communist cause.

So, neutralizing many of the VC's true believers turned out to be a bit more difficult.

True-believing communists were subjected to what CIA officers euphemistically referred to as "the Bell Telephone Hour," (you've probably already noticed that the CIA loves euphemisms), which involved officers tying electrical wires to a suspect's genitals and then sending a surge of power, often from a car battery.

Rape was also a tool routinely used on suspects.

Female suspects were raped or threatened with rape, sometimes with instruments or even animals such as eels and snakes. The torture suspects had to endure was so bad that most confessed, whether they were actual VC or not, with the most hardcore dying of shock or just outright being murdered if they weren't cooperative enough.

And murder was the true name of the game in the Phoenix Program.

Once VC members were identified, the CIA sent the PRUs out to do some more dirty work, or if a VC "hot spot" was identified, the US military was sent in on a "search and destroy" mission (that's a bit less of a euphemism but still somewhat of one, I guess).

It's estimated that the CIA "neutralized" more than 81,000 individuals associated with the VC during the Phoenix Program, which means anything from "turning" a person to the other side to actually killing them.

The official number of those killed by the Phoenix Program is 26,369, the vast majority of which were killed in the military "search and destroy" missions. This leaves 3,426 people who were assassinated either by PRU death squads or actual CIA officers. Granted, the CIA preferred to turn targets, but when that proved futile, or if they couldn't locate a particular target, they would resort to murder.

US Army Lieutenant Vincent Hichiro Okamoto claimed that if certain targets on assassination lists couldn't be found, the hit teams sometimes killed their family members instead.

The End of an Era?

Unlike many other CIA programs and operations, the Phoenix Program was one that the agency admitted existed and claimed to have officially ended in 1972 when the war was coming to an end. Those involved in the Phoenix Program argue that it was very effective, but the reality is that, at best, it merely stalled or slowed the inevitable collapse of South Vietnam and its subsequent incorporation into the North.

Like the other operations discussed so far in this book, the Phoenix Program's existence became public in the US in the early 1970s, leading to Congressional hearings in 1971.

But by that time people were tired of Vietnam and ready to move on. Sure, some of the details that came out were frightening, but most people shrugged it off as a byproduct of a confusing war.

"They won't ever do anything like that again after it was made public," many people said, but the more skeptical among us aren't so convinced. Some say that the Phoenix Program may have been shut down, but the tactics used were kept in place, improved, and then used again in recent years.

Since the CIA maintains secrecy about just about everything, whether that's true or not remains difficult to say. What is clear, though, is that the Phoenix Program was one of the craziest and most brutal operations the CIA has implemented in its relatively short history.

JOHN CHAMBERS AND THE CIA

The number one tool in the CIA's arsenal, or any successful intelligence agency for that matter, is the ability to deceive others. Yes, deception is the key to all CIA missions being successful or not. Whether the deception involves convincing a target that an officer is really someone else or getting millions of people to believe some propaganda, the CIA is always looking for new ways to deceive others.

So, let's take a look at a fascinating individual who used his talent for deception with the CIA.

John Chambers was a well-known Hollywood makeup artist, who in the late 1970s was known for his superb makeup work on the *Star Trek* and *Planet of the Apes* film and TV franchises, among others. But by the late '70s, Chambers felt he'd achieved all he could in Hollywood and began looking for new opportunities and excitement.

That's when the CIA came calling.

Chambers worked for the CIA for years in a sort of real-life *Mission Impossible* scenario, making disguise kits for officers and assets. But Chambers would also later use his numerous Hollywood connections and knowledge of the business to help the Agency complete one particularly fascinating and crazy mission where the lines between Hollywood and espionage were blurred.

In 1979, the world was rocked when the Shah of Iran was overthrown by Islamic militants who wanted a theocracy ruled by Ayatollah Khomeini. The militants eventually took over the US embassy and held 52 Americans hostage for 444 days until the majority were released on January 20, 1981.

But six were rescued earlier, on January 27, 1980, in a joint CIA-Canadian intelligence operation called "The Canadian Caper." You may know a little about this wacky operation from the 2012 film *Argo*, but unfortunately, that movie doesn't feature Chambers or his incredible story very much.

Without Chambers, the operation wouldn't have been a success.

The Real-Life Mission Impossible

John Chambers was born in 1922 to a working-class family in Chicago, Illinois. It was a different time in America. Most boys learned the trade of their fathers, girls usually married at a young age, and only a select few went on to college. Chambers, though, displayed a particular aptitude for art that couldn't be ignored.

Chambers was a natural-born artist, earning money making jewelry and carpets, but his true talent was his ability to accurately reconstruct human anatomy.

When World War II broke out, like most young men, Chambers entered military service. Although the Army needed plenty of healthy young men to fight on the front lines, it also always had

28

its eyes out for people with special talents. Chambers' art background helped him land a position as a dental technician in the Army during the war, which beat fighting in North Africa or having to storm the beaches of Normandy.

After the war, Chambers returned to civilian life with a plethora of potential options, but he chose to do what he loved, and where his true talents were.

Chambers constructed fake ears, noses, breasts, and other appendages for injured soldiers returning home from the war. When the quality of his work began to be noticed, friends and family urged Chambers to try his luck in Hollywood. Film and TV studios were always looking for some good special effects guys, so Chambers should be able to walk right in, they argued.

Well, things may not have been that easy, but not long after, Chambers went to Hollywood and in 1953 he was regularly working in Tinseltown.

After working on many shows for several years, Chambers hit his stride in the 1960s and was finally able to really put his talents to work - talents that the CIA would later find useful. Chambers did makeup, prosthetic limbs and facial features on several sci-fi shows of the late 1960s, including *Lost in Space*, *The Outer Limits*, and *The Munsters*, and he even made the famed pointed ears of Dr. Spock on *Star Trek*!

It was also during the late 1960s that Chambers' work began to imitate reality.

One of Chambers' overlooked jobs was doing makeup and prosthetics for the late '60s, early '70s TV spy show, *Mission: Impossible*. If you aren't familiar with the show, it featured a team of special officers, each with their own skills: a strong man, a femme fatal, a techie, and a makeup and special effects artist. The special effects artist - who was originally played by Martin Landau, and then perhaps somewhat ironically by none other than Spock himself, Leonard Nimoy - was in many ways a reflection of Chambers.

The characters played by Landau and Nimoy on *Mission: Impossible* were noted for creating elaborate disguises to exactly mimic a particular person - either a "bad guy" they were setting up or a "good guy" they were helping to escape, for instance - with elaborate makeup and piece by piece construction of the face. The character would be shown applying the makeup and prosthetics as the show's memorable theme song played, and when it was over - voila! - the character was transformed into the target.

Chambers did all the makeup and prosthetics for those scenes in the pilot episode of the series, and he would later use the same techniques in films such as the *Planet of the Apes* franchise.

The Real-Life *Argo*

Chambers' fame began to precede him and according to famous Hollywood director John Landis, the special effects master also had a sense of humor. In 1997, Landis claimed that Chambers filmed the famous, or infamous, "Patterson Film," which for those of you not into cryptozoology, is the grainy 1967 film that depicts an upright creature strolling through the northern California woods.

The film is often simply called the "Bigfoot Film."

Landis claimed that Chambers built the bigfoot suit with his knowledge of prosthetics and the tools in his shop, but Chambers later stated that he would've done a better job.

Whether Chambers did the "Patterson Film" or not may never be known, but his answer would've been typical of a spook. And based on what we've already seen, and what we'll uncover later in this book, it's not out of the realm of possibility that the CIA would come up with the idea to hoax a bigfoot film. For what reason, we can only guess.

What we do know, though, is that by the late 1970s, John Chambers was officially working for the CIA.

He may have been working for the Agency unofficially when (if?) he did the bigfoot hoax, but it is known that his first official assignments consisted of making disguise kits for CIA officers and assets overseas.

The kits included prosthetics and masks, just like in *Mission: Impossible*, but the plan also involved elaborate backstories and acting lessons. Chambers and his partner Tom Burnman, used their background in the entertainment industry to teach officers to speak with accents and use mannerisms that wouldn't give them away. They also helped set up phony companies to give the officers cover on missions in Laos, Poland, the Soviet Union, and Iran.

It was in Iran where Chambers helped pull off one of the CIA's craziest and most successful missions.

When the hostage crisis happened in Iran, CIA officer Tony Mendez came up with an ambitious plan to rescue six of the American hostages who had managed to get out of the American embassy and into the Canadian embassy.

31

In November 1979, the provisional government in Iran collapsed, which was both good and bad for the hostages. It was bad because the already high level of anarchy on the streets of the capital city of Tehran increased, but it was good because the vacuum in government allowed the CIA to quickly get in and out.

Mendez came up with an elaborate plan he called the "Canadian Caper," which involved John Chambers in a central role. Since Mendez was an expert in exfiltration (getting assets out of a location to safety) and knew the spy tradecraft of fake IDs and makeup quite well, he had already worked with Chambers. Once the Canadian Caper got the green light from Langley (CIA headquarters), the pair immediately got to work.

Chambers and Mendez rented a studio in Hollywood, developed an elaborate backstory, and began compiling their makeup and fake ID kits. Their cover story was that they were filming scenes for a science fiction film based on Roger Zelazny's 1967 novel, *Lord of Light*, which they were calling *Argo*. The film crew would be comprised of six Canadians (the American hostages), a Latin American (Mendez), and an Irishman (Mendez's partner, who's only known as "Julio").

Working closely with members of Canadian intelligence, Mendez and Chambers made authentic-looking Canadian passports and put together a small kit for any touch-up that would be needed on the scene.

After Mendez and Julio quietly made their way into Iran, they went to the Canadian embassy, collected the six hostages, and gave them their new passports. The group then went to the international airport on January 27, 1980, where they flew out of the country on a Swissair flight without a hitch.

32

None of it would've been possible without the skills, connections, and background of makeup artist turned CIA officer, John Chambers.

DID YOU KNOW?

- The full name of Operation CHAOS was actually Operation MHCHAOS. The complete names of all CIA operations were what is known as a cryptonym. The first two letters of the cryptonym usually indicated a geographic area where an operation took place, with "MH" indicating a worldwide operation. The remainder of the cryptonym was usually a clever word that may or may not describe the operation. Other notable geographic cryptonyms were "MK" for the CIA technical services division, "TU" for South Vietnam, and "AM" and "JM" for Cuba.

- The Phoenix Program was part of a bigger program in Vietnam known as Civil Operations and Revolutionary Development Support, or CORDS, from 1967 onward. It is estimated that 700 American CIA and military intelligence officers worked in CORDS and the Phoenix Program, although the lines between the two were often blurred.

- A right-wing product of both COINTELPRO and Operation CHAOS was a survivalist militia known as the Secret Army Organization (SAO). The SAO, whose leader Jerry Lynn Davis was a CIA asset in the early 1960s, targeted anti-war leaders in the late 1960s with violence, intimidation, and blackmail.

- Robert Barron was another CIA master of disguise and makeup artist. After going undercover at a medical conference in 1983, Barron decided to change careers and make prosthetic limbs and appendages for those suffering from disfigurement due to car accidents, cancer, or birth defects.

- The magazine *Ramparts*, which proved to be a constant thorn in the CIA's side, ran from 1962 until 1975. Despite its decidedly left-wing stances, some notable conservatives got their starts with *Ramparts*, including David Horowitz and Brit Hume.

A TRUE FALSE FLAG OPERATION

At this point, you should know that things aren't as they always seem, which is the strength of the CIA and other intelligence organizations around the world. The CIA became powerful through deception, demonstrating that it was perfectly willing to take that deception to some extreme levels. With this in mind, you shouldn't be faulted if you question just about every major event in the world.

For instance, recent poisonous gas attacks in Syria were first reported by the mainstream American press as being the work of Syrian President Bashar al-Assad, but now reports have surfaced that it may have been the work of ISIS affiliates. Those who still argue that al-Assad was behind the attacks, such as the "former" CIA officers who work as commentators at CNN and MSNBC (the remnants of Operation Mockingbird?), claim that ISIS would have no reason to attack people who are opposed to the current regime.

But more cynical people state that it looks like a very basic "false flag attack."

A false flag attack or operation is done by one country or organization to make it look like another country or organization was the perpetrator. When Germany invaded Poland to start

World War II, it was done under the pretense that Polish troops fired on a German border checkpoint. The Soviets also performed a false flag attack on Finland in 1939 and the Japanese used a false flag attack as the pretext for their invasion of Manchuria in 1931.

The key to a good false flag operation is for it to gain sympathy for one's cause and for it to be nearly undetectable.

Many historians believe the arson of the Reichstag (parliament building) in Germany in 1933 was a false flag by the Nazi Party. A communist was arrested, tried, convicted, and executed for the fire, but many believe it was a well-done Nazi operation.

The sinking of the USS *Maine* in Havana, Cuba harbor in 1889 is also believed by many to have been a false flag operation carried out by the US government to create a *casus belli* to go to war against Spain for control of Cuba.

If the Reichstag fire and the bombing of *Maine* were false flag operations, they were more or less textbook examples of how they should be done. The public will never know for sure if they were and anyone involved got away scot-free.

More than likely, the CIA bigwigs were reading up on the Reichstag fire and the *Maine* bombing when they came up with their own false flag operation - Operation Northwoods.

Castro Has to Go

When Fidel Castro became Cuba's dictator in 1959 through a revolution and guerilla insurgency, most Americans, including the leaders of the country, didn't know what to expect. He claimed to be a reformer and the previous leader of the country,

Fulgencio Batista, was more or less a caricature of a corrupt Latin American dictator, so many were willing to take a wait-and-see approach to Castro.

The Mafia liked Batista because he worked with them and the CIA liked him because he was corruptible, but others in the American government weren't so sad to see him leave.

It didn't take long for it to become apparent that Castro was a true Marxist/communist. He quickly began nationalizing all foreign businesses in Cuba and started cozying up to the Soviet Union.

This was too much for many in the US government, including the shot callers at the CIA.

When Democrat John F. Kennedy won the presidential election in 1960, he was a fresh new face on what was a political scene dominated by older men. The reality, though, was that he continued many of the policies of his Republican predecessor, Dwight D. Eisenhower.

Kennedy was moderate on domestic and racial issues but tough on communism globally, which is how he became entangled in more than one CIA operation.

When Castro took power in Cuba, the US military and CIA incessantly lobbied for Kennedy to get rid of the man in the fatigues with the cigar and beard who was just 90 miles south of Florida. For the most part, Kennedy agreed, and he even authorized the failed Bay of Pigs invasion in 1961.

But short of a full-scale invasion of Cuba, there was only so much Kennedy was willing to do. The CIA, on the other hand, had far fewer restraints than the American president when it came to getting rid of Castro.

And as you already know, the CIA had a large arsenal of tricks it could use to get the job done.

The idea of Operation Northwoods was proposed by the Department of Defense in a 1962 document titled, "Justification for U.S. Military Intervention in Cuba (TS)." The plan was for the CIA to use its plethora of assets in the US and Latin America to carry out one or more false flag attacks that could be used to justify a full-scale invasion of Cuba, with some of the plans being a bit crazier than others.

Battleground Miami

The CIA had many analysts contribute to ideas for Operation Northwoods, and they came up with three potential scenarios.

The first would involve launching attacks on the American Navy base in Guantanamo Bay, Cuba. CIA officers disguised as Cuban soldiers would attack the base with minimal firepower, in the hopes of leaving only minor casualties and damages but meanwhile creating the cover needed for a US invasion. President Kennedy could go to the United Nations and the international press and point out that Cuba did in fact represent a clear and present danger to the United States and that therefore, an American invasion was justified.

Another potential scenario involved CIA and US Special Forces conducting attacks on Jamaica and Trinidad and Tobago, once again making it look like it was the work of either pro-Cuban communist revolutionaries or Cuban commandos. The thought in this scenario was that since those countries were former British colonies, and still were members of the British

Commonwealth, that the United Kingdom would support a US invasion of Cuba.

Any help was needed, especially when it came to diplomacy.

But the craziest scenario involved the CIA conducting bombings, kidnappings, and assassinations on American soil.

The CIA planned to do several terrorist attacks on American soil, primarily in the Miami, Florida area where most of the Cuban expat community lived. Yes, the CIA planned to turn Miami into a slaughterhouse to start a war with Cuba. And if that isn't bad enough, the scenario gets even crazier when you consider who the CIA's Miami targets would've been.

Since the CIA was attempting to frame Cuba, they were going to target anti-Castro Cuban dissidents in southern Florida, many of whom were CIA assets! It actually would've been pretty easy since the CIA knew where these people lived, where they worked, and many of their strengths and weaknesses. The plan called for assassinating a few dissident leaders, sinking some boats with Cuban refugees, and possibly hijacking a plane or two.

Nothing big, just run-of-the-mill spy turned terrorist stuff!

And if that didn't work, the CIA would also bring their terror campaign to the heartland to make sure Joe and Jane Smith were on their side in the war against Cuba.

As much as President Kennedy may have hated Castro, Operation Northwoods was just too much. He shot down the idea in March 1962, which rankled the CIA. Some say that when Kennedy rejected Operation Northwoods for its sheer craziness, he made himself a target of the CIA.

Unfortunately, we'll probably never know the complete truth of the role, if any, the CIA and Operation Northwoods played in Kennedy's assassination.

SEX, DRUGS, ROCK N' ROLL, AND THE CIA

We've seen how the CIA has had a long history of doing operations that were unethical, illegal, and most would say, immoral. These crazy operations involved spying on American citizens, torturing and killing non-Americans, and developing an overly cozy relationship with the mainstream media and Hollywood.

This next case demonstrates just how far the CIA was willing to go to achieve its ends.

As the Cold War was raging in the early 1950s, the American military and the CIA were looking for every advantage they could get, no matter how much those advantages would defeat the purpose of the American effort of defending freedom. The bigwigs in the Army's Biological Warfare Laboratories, along with CIA officer Sidney Gottlieb, looked to their current and former enemies for inspiration.

Gottlieb was impressed with Nazi mind control experiments in World War II as well as those supposedly being done by the Soviets at the time. With his background in chemistry and support from CIA director Allen Dulles and the Army brass, Gottlieb was given the green light to begin his own mind control experiments, dubbed Project MKUltra, and its notable sub-operation, Operation Midnight Climax, in 1953.

What took place next was perhaps the craziest and most influential of all CIA operations.

The CIA dosed perhaps thousands of unwitting people with the strong psychedelic drug lysergic acid diethylamide - better known as LSD or "acid" - in order to post subliminal suggestions, or "triggers," in the minds of the subjects. Later, a "controller" would then use the trigger to get the subject to do various things, from collecting information to possibly even murder.

Sex also became a major part of MKUltra, as a way to get subjects to let their guards down, especially after they had been given a dose of LSD or other psychedelic drugs.

MKUltra took place at a time when so few people knew what LSD was that it was technically legal. However, by the time the operation was in full swing in the 1960s, things had drastically changed.

Some say that MKUltra was the true force behind the counterculture movement, while others say that despite the CIA's claims that the program was discontinued in 1973, there are still programmed assets and officers among us who are patiently waiting for their triggers.

Not a Trip You'd Want to Take

Long before the hippies of America were tuning in and dropping out on acid and other psychedelic drugs, a Swiss chemist named Albert Hoffman invented the drug in a laboratory in 1938. After Hoffman's discovery, LSD remained a relatively unknown and legal drug for some time.

Yes, LSD was legal until 1968, so before that time, the CIA had plenty of leeway with its use of the drug when Project MKUltra got underway in 1953. The Agency could legally purchase LSD, which it did by buying the world's supply for $240,000, and it also had plenty of its own chemists to make more if need be.

And since the CIA used plenty of doses, there were plenty of chances for enterprising young chemists to perfect their craft under the watchful eyes of the CIA.

But the thing is, since LSD was such a new drug in 1953, the officers of Project MKUltra didn't know how much to give subjects or what the effects would be. So, when the program was finally ready to go, Gottlieb had officers administer large, powerful doses of LSD to unsuspecting subjects.

LSD is a powerful drug that can give the user feelings of great euphoria or incredible despair, all in the same "trip", as a single session of being on the drug is called. In high-level doses, users often experience intense hallucinations that can be very frightening, especially if the user doesn't even know what they are on.

And that was basically MKUltra in a nutshell. Test subjects were surreptitiously dosed so that when the trip "kicked in," they were unaware of what was happening. The Army and the CIA saw great potential in LSD. They believed it could be used in interrogations to break the prisoner's will to resist, and it could also be used in more intricate operations.

Gottlieb believed that LSD could be administered to subjects who would then be "programmed" by CIA psychologists with suggestions. The subject could then be "activated" at a later time with a word, series of words, or a mnemonic device that acted as a "trigger."

So, LSD was given to patients at mental hospitals and prisoners without their consent, which although illegal, would hardly raise more than an eyebrow in 1953. The results showed that the dosed individuals routinely broke down and told the officers whatever they wanted to hear, which for the CIA was good news, but for Gottlieb, it didn't demonstrate LSD's true potential.

For that, he would need to secretly dose professionals with military and intelligence backgrounds.

People with military and intelligence backgrounds already had the requisite training to be assassins, but they still possessed a moral compass and free will, both of which Gottlieb hoped to eliminate through heavy doses of surreptitiously administered LSD. This was done by giving it to CIA officers and military officers in their coffee or food. Civilians were also given strong doses of the hallucinogen without their knowledge.

One military officer unknowingly dosed was a captain in the Army's Chemical Corps named Frank Olson.

The Show Must Go On

Frank Olson was a pretty smart guy and a true patriot, which was exactly the sort of person the CIA was recruiting in the early 1950s. Olson earned a PhD in bacteriology from the University of Wisconsin in 1938 and then served in the Army before working for the military during World War II as a civilian contractor.

After World War II, the CIA learned of Olson's work on chemical and biological weapons and recruited him to join. Believing that he was defending his country, Olson enthusiastically climbed the ranks of the CIA, becoming the head of the Special Operations Division (MK) in 1952.

Olson's first major project was Operation Artichoke, which involved administering chemicals to a subject being interrogated and to biological officers. After learning of some of the extreme interrogation methods the Chinese and North Koreans used on captured American and Allied soldiers during the Korean War (1950-1952) - which involved beatings, threats, sleep deprivation, and starvation, among other tactics—the CIA thought they could do even better.

Before long, Operation Artichoke evolved into Project MKUltra and Olson became one of its first victims.

By November 1953, Olson had grown disillusioned with the tactics Gottlieb and the CIA were using in MKUltra. Perhaps sensing this, Gottlieb summoned Olson and nine other CIA officers and military officers associated with the bioweapons program and MKUltra to a Maryland wilderness retreat on November 18.

But Olson and the others weren't in rural Maryland for rest and relaxation; Gottlieb made sure that the men endured the most bizarre and scariest experience of their lives!

Gottlieb dosed the men with LSD and only later told them that they were given a "truth serum." We'll probably never know the amount or strength of the dose the men were administered, but since LSD was stronger and unregulated at the time, it's safe to assume that it was an extremely strong dose.

After the men spent the weekend losing their grip on reality, they were all unceremoniously allowed to return to their homes. According to his wife, Olson never really came off the trip. He told his wife that people were following him and he also said he was going to resign. Then Olson capriciously changed his mind and decided to keep working with the CIA and the bioweapons program.

But by then it was probably too late.

Olson met with some Army brass and a CIA officer involved with MKUltra in New York City on November 24. The group gathered at a hotel in Manhattan, but of course, the details of their meetings will forever be a mystery. What is known, though, is that at 2.00 a.m. on November 28, Olson leapt from the window of his room to his death.

One theory is that Olson was assassinated out of fear that he was going to spill the beans on Project MKUltra, while the more probable theory is that the high dose of LSD, he was administered caused psychosis that resulted in suicide.

Either way though, Olson's death could've been a setback for MKUltra, but as far as Gottlieb was concerned, the show had to go on.

Sex and Drugs

For many organizations, the loss of Olson would have signaled serious problems and the probable end of the operation, but for the CIA and Gottlieb, it represented new opportunities. Olson was a potential problem, so with him gone, no matter how that happened, the CIA could concentrate on new mind-control experiments in MKUltra.

In 1954, Gottlieb decided to bring in officers with the Federal Narcotics Bureau (the forerunner of the Drug Enforcement Agency) to help with his ambitious new sub-operation of Project MKUltra - Operation Midnight Climax.

If you're thinking the name of this operation sounds very sexual, you're right. I guess the CIA does have a bit of a sense of humor, although this extremely crazy operation wasn't so funny to the men caught in its net.

Operation Midnight Climax began in 1954 in the San Francisco and New York metropolitan areas as an expansion of the initial MKUltra experiments, but instead of dosing CIA and military unwittingly with LSD, hapless men were targeted. The CIA used sex workers to lure men back to CIA safehouses, where they would be clandestinely dosed with LSD and other drugs either before or after sex. The CIA would often watch from behind a one-way glass mirror.

They weren't watching for any kinky reasons necessarily, but more to catch the men in comprising acts since some were reported to be influential in their communities.

In addition to sexual blackmail, CIA officers used the sex workers to elicit important information from the men and place suggestions in the men's minds while they were under the influence of LSD.

By the late 1950s, the CIA was regularly dosing random people in several major cities and even expanded their operations to Canada. With the help of Canadian intelligence and British psychologist Donald Ewen Cameron, Project MKUltra experimented on hundreds of patients at Montreal's McGill University from 1957 through 1964.

The patients thought they were being treated for schizophrenia and other severe forms of mental illness, but instead, Cameron did many devious things to them, such as placing them in comas for days, weeks, or even months. Cameron would then use audiotapes to place suggestions in the comatose patients' minds.

MKUltra was supposedly reduced in scale in the late 1960s and officially discontinued in 1973 as the Church committee began investigating Operation Mockingbird.

The CIA has never revealed how many American citizens became real-life Manchurian candidates during Project MKUltra, but it is believed to be in the hundreds and possibly thousands.

Even more frightening? We'll probably never know how many people have been assassinated by those real-life Manchurian candidates.

THE DRUG SMUGGLING CIA?
PART ONE

The Vietnam War was probably the messiest, most confusing war in American history. Most Americans really didn't understand what was going on over there - including people who were both for and against the war. As we've already shown, it was much more complex and brutal than merely helping the South Vietnamese put down a communist insurgency in their country.

North Vietnam was constantly feeding supplies to the VC through the Ho Chi Minh Trail, which snaked through both North and South Vietnam and into parts of Cambodia and Laos.

Cambodia and Laos were also fighting off communist insurgencies, and by the late 1960s, there were American military advisors and CIA officers in both of those countries.

In Laos, the CIA supported the Hmong people, who were an ethnic group that lived in the northern mountains of the country. The Hmong were opposed to the Laotian communists and fought against the North Vietnamese when they invaded Laos, so the CIA figured the Hmong were the perfect allies.

The Hmong proved to be good fighters and wanted very little for their service. They just asked to have relative autonomy in their mountainous homes and to live as they had for centuries.

They also wanted to be free to grow and sell their poppy plants.

Poppy is the key ingredient used to make opiates such as opium and heroin, which meant that those fields were very valuable. Although the CIA has denied any involvement with drug trafficking, the evidence clearly shows that several CIA officers were involved in trafficking opium and heroin in and out of the Golden Triangle region of southeast Asia (the borderland of Thailand, Laos, and Myanmar/Burma).

The CIA admits that some of its officers *may* have been involved in the drug smuggling, but claims the amounts were small and that there was never an official drug smuggling program.

So, were the CIA trafficking drugs during the Vietnam War, in just another crazy CIA mission? Or was it just a few crazy CIA officers getting carried away? It's for you to decide!

Air America

We've seen how part of the CIA's operational success has been setting up front businesses or groups. This gives the CIA the look of normalcy and allows them to manipulate civilians and potentially use them to take the fall if things go south.

This sort of setup enables the CIA to invoke what's known as "plausible deniability," which is where officers can claim, truthfully or not, to have no knowledge of a particular operation, thereby limiting their legal liability. In the case of Golden

Triangle drug smuggling, the civilian air transportation company, Air America, gave the CIA plausible deniability.

Air America originally began as a Chinese civilian airline called Civil Air Transport. After China fell to the communists, the CIA bought CAT outright in 1950 and renamed it Air America. On its face, Air America was a civilian transport company that could deliver people and goods to isolated locations around East Asia. In reality, it was run by spooks who were constantly gathering intelligence and using the planes to conduct top-secret missions.

And by the late 1960s, those operations included moving weapons and materials in and out of Laos for General Vang Pao of the Royal Lao Army.

Pao was a man who was known for cutting corners and being a bit shady, to say the least, but he was also a Hmong and was therefore believed to be trustworthy. At least, that's what CIA officer Theodore Shackley believed.

Shackley was a career intelligence officer who moved his way up the ranks of the fairly new CIA in the 1950s and '60s. After working on Operation Mongoose (we'll get to that crazy operation a bit later), Shackley was made the CIA station chief in Laos in 1966. He was tasked with carrying out the "secret war" in Laos against communist forces, which meant he had great leeway with his methods.

Shackley used intelligence and methods gleaned from the Phoenix Program and basically became a law onto himself in Laos. He was known to bend just about every rule there was (and as we've seen so far, the CIA didn't really care about rules anyway), especially when it came to General Pao.

You see, General Pao knew how to get results, so Shackley let him do pretty much whatever he wanted. This included using Air America to smuggle opium out of northern Laos and through the Laotian military base in Long Tieng.

What happened after the opium made it to the base, and how much the CIA knew about it, is still a matter of debate.

Guns, Drugs, and Death in the Golden Triangle

The Laotian Army's biggest problem was getting weapons. The US supported them to a certain extent, but theoretically, all government funding is supposed to go through Congress and by the late '60s, it was getting harder for lawmakers to justify spending more money on the Vietnam War, especially if it involved expanding the war into Laos.

So, General Pao's idea was simple: sell the opium for hard cash and use the currency to buy weapons. There's no debate that Pao and the Laotian Army smuggled and sold opium, it's just a matter of what the CIA knew and how much they were involved in the smuggling, if at all.

There's almost no way the CIA didn't know that opium and heroin smuggling was taking place on Air America flights. It's the CIA's purpose to know things about people, places, and countries, and since they were so heavily involved in Laos at the time, it's pretty safe to assume that they knew exactly what Pao was doing.

Then there were the interviews given by former Air America pilots who claimed they knew they were moving drugs on behalf of Pao.

And there's also the curious case of CIA officer Anthony Poshepny, also known as "Tony Poe."

Poshepny was a truly interesting character and an authentic badass.

He served in the Marines during World War II, fighting at Iwo Jima, where he was wounded, but that was just the beginning of Poshepny's colorful career in intelligence and warfare.

Poshepny specialized in guerilla activities in East Asia, helping train anti-communist guerilla fighters throughout Asia after World War II as part of the CIA.

After fighting in almost every jungle and mountain chain in Southeast Asia during the 1950s, Poshepny was sent to Laos in 1961 to help train the Hmong anti-communist forces and to create a network of guerillas that the Americans could utilize in their fight. It's important to point out that Poshepny's involvement in Laos was long before any American official involvement in southeast Asia, which gave the Marine turned CIA officer plenty of latitude with which to run his operations according to his own rules.

Poshepny paid his Hmong fighters to reach high kill counts and to bring him the ears of those they killed as proof. He also fought alongside the Hmong when he was supposed to be an "advisor," getting into the grizzly nature of the war by severing the heads, ears, and digits of his communist enemies, and then often clandestinely placing them in enemy camps.

Because of all this, even the CIA saw Poshepny as a bit of a loose cannon. He was extracted from Laos in 1970 and is said to have later been the inspiration for the character Colonel Kurtz in the 1979 film *Apocalypse Now* (another example of the blurred line between the CIA and Hollywood?).

Poshepny later claimed that the CIA knew about General Pao's opium and heroin smuggling, but that it turned a blind eye to the action.

So, if Air America was used by General Pao to smuggle drugs to raise funds for the Lao Army, where did all the opium and heroin go?

The answer to this question and the details surrounding it remain even murkier than the entire Air America operation. Those who argue the CIA played a more active role in the drug smuggling say that officers moved the drugs to different locations around the world, including the United States, where it was dispersed to their underworld contacts.

It's a well-known fact that the CIA protected Corsican mob heroin networks after World War II, so it's reasonable to believe at least some of the heroin made it to the Corsicans in Europe. It's also thought that American organized crime groups such as the Cosa Nostra and Meyer Lansky's network got a fair amount of the dope, which they distributed around the country.

If you believe the CIA only turned a blind eye to the smuggling, then it was probably several different people and networks acting independently who dispersed the heroin throughout the world.

It may never be known if the CIA played an active role in heroin smuggling in the Golden Triangle, or if they just looked the other way when it happened. Either way, the CIA's involvement in the Golden Triangle in the 1960s and '70s helped pave the way for a drug crisis that would reach epidemic proportions.

CATS MAKE GREAT PETS, NOT-SO-GREAT SPIES

Since ancient times, cats have been among humans' favorite pets. In those early days, cats helped people by killing dangerous vermin but over time they became valued as companions almost as much as dogs.

Cats are cute, soft, smart, interesting, and they *sometimes* reciprocate the love we give them. But cat lovers generally don't mind the aloof nature of their feline friends; it's just the way they are and part of what makes them a desirable pet.

Those of you who know this, also know that training a cat to do much of anything can be next to impossible. The phrase "it's like herding cats" is known worldwide for a reason - because it's true!

Sure, some of you reading this may have taught your cats to sit, shake, or do some other type of trick, but those are exceptions and exceptions only prove the rule. Cats may make great pets, but they'll never be dogs, which is fine with most cat owners.

But someone should have told this to the CIA's Directorate of Science and Technology in the late 1960s.

The Directorate was tasked with coming up with new ways to spy on America's enemies and gather intelligence, eventually developing some incredible state-of-the-art listening and communication devices. We've seen how the Directorate of Science and Technology used LSD and other drugs during Project MKUltra, but they also were responsible for developing some amazing technology.

The CIA developed the highly used lithium-ion battery and was also responsible for advancing radar and satellite technology. In many ways, the Directorate of Science and Technology was the inspiration for James Bond and other spy films and TV series of the late 1960s, where the main character was aided by an arsenal of cool gadgets that were clearly ahead of the times.

So, the CIA had some smart people working for them in the 1960s, which makes this next mission all that more humorous.

The geniuses in the CIA's Directorate of Science and Technology thought it'd be a *purrrrfect* idea to implant listening devices in cats.

And the techies came up with a pretty cool device, but the reality is that they just didn't understand the basic nature of cats. I guess the people in the Directorate of Science and Technology were raised in homes without pets because if they had been, they would've known you can't teach a cat to be a spy!

An Eager Operation

The Directorate of Science and Technology was asked to devise a new and effective way to spy on people. It was allotted more than $20 million for the project, but the best they could come up with was Operation Acoustic Kitty.

With a name that ridiculous, everyone should've known that the project was bound to be a failure. So why did some CIA nerds think a feline secret officer was a good idea and how was it supposed to work?

The answer to the first question is quite logical. Since the CIA is always about deception, and deception often involves blending into one's surroundings, what better way to do this than through a cat? Cats are a ubiquitous part of urban landscapes in many cities, so the potential target of a CIA mission would be unlikely to notice Fluffy walking around nearby. In fact, if the target was a cat lover, they may even bend over to pet the cat!

Okay, so it makes sense on some level to use a cat to get close to a potential target, but how was the cat supposed to get any usable intelligence?

Well, for that the CIA employed veterinarians who surgically implanted a microphone inside the cat's ear, an antenna along its spine, and a transmitter and power supply on its chest.

This was all state-of-the-art technology for the 1960s, but not everyone was on board with Operation Acoustic Kitty's ethical implications, such as the former assistant to the CIA director, Victor Marchetti, who called it "Frankenkitty."

Once the kitty was rigged up, it was time to test the creation in a CIA lab.

Surprisingly, the cat performed quite well in lab tests and actually responded to orders, to a certain extent. At least, it performed well enough to do live exercises away from the lab.

In those tests, the cat acted as any normal cat would. It became preoccupied with other animals, chased birds, and generally didn't get close to the trial target. Still, since the CIA had invested so much in the bizarre operation, the decision was made to greenlight the project.

Operation Kitty Goes Live

When it finally came time to put Fluffy in the field (real name redacted, of course!) her CIA handlers were anxious to pull it off. It could've been a real boon for their careers and possibly the next step in cybernetic evolution.

The targets of Fluffy's first mission were two guys seated on a park bench near the USSR embassy in Washington, D.C., although it isn't clear if they were Soviet spies or just two random people; the only published reports don't say and apparently no one associated with the mission wanted to speak about it.

The cat was released and what happened next became the subject of a macabre legend.

According to one report, the cat immediately made a b-line for the street and was hit and killed by a car, forever ending Fluffy's short and inauspicious spook career, taking Operation Acoustic Kitty with her.

This version of the mission was later disputed by the former director of Science and Technology, Robert Wallace, who admitted Operation Acoustic Kitty was a failure but said that the cat lived a long life and had the communication devices surgical removed from her body.

Apparently, the CIA continued Operation Acoustic Kitty with other cats before finally shutting the program down in 1967.

Perhaps one of the most amusing parts of this very amusing operation was the memorandum on the mission.

The report read, "The program would not lend itself in a practical sense to our highly specialized needs."

But the report also noted the scientific success of the operation:

"This is in itself a remarkable achievement. Knowing that cats can be trained to move short distances, we see no reason to believe that a cat cannot be similarity trained to approach however, the environmental and security factors in using this technique in a real foreign situation force us to conclude that, for our purposes, it would not be practical."

Hmmm, really?

It took the CIA millions of dollars, countless man-hours, and plenty of frustration to learn something that any cat owner would've been glad to tell them...

Cats make great pets, not-so-great spies!

DID YOU KNOW?

- Among the people who claim to have been a subject/target of Project MKUltra was notable counterculture writer, Ken Kesey. Kesey is best known as the author of *One Flew Over the Cuckoo's Nest*, which he claims was based on his experiences as a subject of CIA LSD experiments at the Menlo Park Veteran's Hospital in Menlo Park, California. Counterculture and acid guru Timothy Leary is another high-profile person who was suspected to be connected to Project MKUltra. Before becoming a hippy and drug guru, Leary ran experiments at Harvard University and the state prison in Concord, California where the effects of LSD and psilocybin (a hallucinogenic compound found naturally in some mushrooms) on individuals was studied. Both of these men would later be instrumental in spreading the use of hallucinogenic drugs in the counterculture movement.

- The 1985 action film, *Invasion U.S.A.*, which starred Chuck Norris, is yet another example of Hollywood reflecting a CIA mission. The plot involved communists who committed a series of terrorist attacks around the US, but primarily in Miami, to create civil discord. The movie was obviously influenced by Operation Northwoods to a certain extent.

- Anthony Poshepny was often known by his alias, Tony Poe. Poshepny wasn't just passing through when he worked for the CIA in Southeast Asia, as he married a Hmong woman and started a family in Thailand. He lived in Thailand - presumably while still working for the CIA - until the 1990s when he moved back to the US with his family.

- The story of Air America was first made public in a 1978 nonfiction book, *Air America*, but it was the 1990 film of the same name starring Mel Gibson and Robert Downey Junior that made the airline world famous. The film features Air America pilots trafficking guns and drugs.

- The Gold Triangle comprises about 367,000 square miles on the borders of Thailand, Laos, and Myanmar. After the anti-communist forces lost in the Chinese Civil War in 1949, some crossed into the Golden Triangle region to start the tradition of growing, smuggling and selling opium for arms.

SO, THERE REALLY WAS SOMETHING TO THAT ANTI-VAX THING IN PAKISTAN

When the 9-11 terrorist attacks happened, they shook the United States to its core and shocked the world. It was a black swan event that no one saw coming, including the CIA, and it threatened to destabilize the American economy and political system. In addition to the thousands who died in the attacks, it led to protracted wars and occupations of Afghanistan and Iraq, which left thousands of Americans dead as well as tens of thousands more Afghanis, Iraqis, and military personnel from around the world who were aligned with the US.

As soon as the attacks happened, Osama bin Laden, the leader of the Islamic terrorist group al-Qaeda, claimed credit. Osama bin Laden immediately became public enemy number one in the US, grabbing the infamous top spot on the FBI's Ten Most Wanted list and being featured in countless newscasts, documentaries, and crime "tip" shows like *America's Most Wanted* and *Unsolved Mysteries*.

But no matter how much attention the hunt for bin Laden was given, the terrorist mastermind couldn't be found.

Planning for the international manhunt well ahead of time, bin Laden began his run from the American authorities as soon as the 9-11 attacks took place. He moved through a network of al-Qaeda and Taliban safehouses in Afghanistan before crossing the border into Pakistan in early 2002. He eventually settled in the northwest Pakistani city of Abbottabad in 2005, where he lived until he was killed in a combined CIA-Navy SEAL operation in 2011.

The actual killing of bin Laden wasn't necessarily crazy, but the operation that led to him being identified was. It involved the collection of children's DNA in Abbottabad under the guise that they were being vaccinated for hepatitis B.

As you probably know, worldwide vaccinations for COVID-19 have been ongoing since their approval. At the time of writing, many people have received one of the available vaccines, but almost as many in some places, or even more in others, have refused. Experts refer to the phenomena of large numbers of people refusing to get vaccinated as "vaccine hesitancy," which stems from several reasons.

Some people have medical reasons not to get vaccinated.

Others have religious objections to vaccinations in general.

Still, others have a general distrust of the government and any vaccines it supports.

Those in the final category point to several historical cases where governments have used unwitting citizens as guinea pigs, or as dupes in elaborate ruses such as the operation to capture and kill Osama bin Laden.

Those in the CIA say the operation was worth it, but others point out that the vaccine trick created a lot of tension between

Pakistan and the United States and lowered people's trust in vaccines in general.

A CIA Asset?

Osama bin Laden was born into a wealthy, privileged Saudi family and could have lived the life of an Arab playboy, but instead chose the path of religious extremism. When the Soviets invaded Afghanistan in 1979 in support of the socialist government in that country, which was threatened with collapse by Islamic guerillas known as the Mujahideen, it started the bloody Soviet-Afghan War.

Feeling the call of his religion, and being a young man in search of adventure, bin Laden traveled to Afghanistan to join the Mujahideen, using his family's money to bankroll his activities.

This is where things get a little confusing and a bit ironic as far as the CIA is concerned.

At this point in the book, it should be clear that the CIA of the Cold War era was anti-communist and that they were willing to go to extreme and crazy lengths to carry out that mission.

This is where our unbelievable story of the phony CIA vaccinations in Pakistan begins to get crazy.

The CIA initiated Operation Cyclone after the Soviet invasion of Afghanistan to funnel money to Mujahideen through the Pakistani Inter-Services Intelligence (ISI). The CIA claims that funds and training rarely went directly to the Mujahideen and that bin Laden was never involved directly in any of their operations, but it is known that some of the terrorist leader's latter associates *were* funded directly by the CIA.

For example, there is the case of notorious double officer Ali Mohammed.

Ali Mohammed was an Egyptian-born Islamic radical who was also an asset for the CIA and US Army intelligence. Mohammad would train bin Laden in the early 1990s to carry out the type of attacks for which al-Qaeda became infamous.

It was in this convoluted web of cloak and dagger and changing alliances that bin Laden's worldview was formed; it was also where he learned his terror and evasion tactics. It should come as no surprise that bin Laden was able to avoid capture for so long because he was familiar with CIA tactics.

But as much as bin Laden may have known that the CIA wasn't above doing some crazy things, he never imagined the outlandish plan they had to capture him.

We're Here to Help You

The CIA wasn't getting very far finding bin Laden through its worldwide network of spies, so it resorted to the old-fashioned way of getting intel - torture.

All the waterboarding and threats the CIA was doing on prisoners in Guantanamo Bay, Cuba finally paid off when some detainees began slowly but surely leaking information about bin Laden's courier system. Since bin Laden knew all about CIA tracking technologies and methods, he used human couriers to relate information and orders from around the world to the three-story compound he was living in with his family in Abbottabad, Pakistan. CIA satellites and further intelligence all but confirmed bin Laden was living in the compound, but they still had to make sure, which is where this crazy vaccine idea was hatched.

The details of what happened next, as is the case with so many CIA operations, are disputed and unclear to a certain extent, but it appears the CIA recruited a Pakistani doctor named Shakil Afridi to be the main asset in the operation.

Or was he recruited to be a patsy?

In the spring of 2011, Afridi and the CIA set up a fake hepatitis B vaccine program for the children of Abbottabad. They began by giving the "vaccine" to children in the poorer neighborhoods of the city before making their way to bin Laden's neighborhood to not arouse suspicions.

The ruse worked as the people in the compound allowed Afridi to "vaccinate" all the children present. The vaccine was actual surreptitiously taken DNA samples, which were then compared to one of bin Laden's sisters who had died in 2010 in Boston, Massachusetts.

The DNA of the children was a match and the rest, as they say, was history.

But the ending of this story wasn't so happy or simple for all parties involved. After the excitement of the news of bin Laden's death had subsided and the details of the fake vaccine were revealed, the government of Pakistan wasn't too happy. They were angry that they hadn't been alerted to such a large and complex operation taking place on their soil (which is understandable from the Americans' point of view because officers in the ISI were actually helping bin Laden). Pakistani officials were also angry about the deception of the fake vaccine.

It's one thing for spies to pull shenanigans on each other, but when they start involving citizens, and many children in this case, then that's an entirely other matter. But Pakistan had little leverage in this case. All they could do was arrest the one Pakistani involved in the crazy operation, Afridi.

Afridi was arrested attempting to leave Pakistan days after the raid. He was tried for cooperating with an anti-government warlord and when he beat that charge, the Pakistani government charged, tried, and convicted him for the murder of one of his patients.

The Pakistani government has since offered to exchange him for a Pakistani woman convicted of terrorism in the US, but they've received no reply.

It looks like Afridi was just another CIA patsy after all.

Many experts point out that perhaps the craziest aspect of this operation was the vaccine hesitancy it's created in Pakistan; low levels of vaccination do exist in that country. It's difficult to say for sure how much this crazy CIA operation contributed to global vaccine hesitancy, but it likely has been a factor.

THE CIA COULDN'T KILL CASTRO

We've seen so far how the CIA did what it wanted, when it wanted, and essentially made up its own rules. The CIA was, for the most part, an organization that operated outside the laws that most people and governments around the world followed and did whatever it needed to get the job done.

But even the CIA had limits.

There's an unwritten rule among intelligence agencies that heads of state are off-limits for assassination. It isn't so much that the CIA and its rival organizations around the world respect world leaders; it's more that killing them just isn't good for business. Assassinations tend to be messy and lead to many conspiracy theories, which is exactly the type of thing the CIA doesn't want.

The CIA hates how it is continually implicated in the Kennedy assassination because whether it's true or not, it sheds light on some of the Agency's nefarious activities.

Of course, though, there are always exceptions and one of the biggest ones is the fatigue-wearing, cigar-smoking dictator from just 90 miles south of Florida: Fidel Castro.

Fidel Castro proved to be such a thorn in the side of President Kennedy, and later American presidents, that there were supposedly 638 missions to kill the Latin American dictator.

Yes, you read the correctly, *638 assassination attempts*!

Although not all those attempts have been proven or admitted to by the CIA, it's a pretty crazy number when you think about it. It's amazing to think that the CIA, or any intelligence agency for that matter, would go around trying to kill a foreign head of state, regardless of how much of a despot he was. Yet here the CIA attempted it numerous times.

So, what does this say about the CIA?

Was the CIA truly an evil and bloodthirsty organization, as some argue?

Or were the CIA's abilities exaggerated and it bordered on incompetent, as others say when they point out every failed attempt after failed attempt?

Well, that's up for you to decide, but there's no doubt that the CIA's attempts to kill Castro were as ridiculous as any of the missions profiled in this book.

Operation Mongoose

We've seen already how the CIA had no qualms about being a law unto itself, and we've also seen how, in the early 1960s, it particularly hated Fidel Castro. Sure, it was strongly opposed to his political ideology, but the CIA also had a personal problem with Castro.

Who did he think he was, running his own country free of US government involvement just 90 miles from Florida? He had to be stopped.

And things only got more personal the more the CIA and American military tried, and failed, to remove Castro.

The campaign to remove Castro from power, and later to kill him, officially began in March 1960 when then-President Eisenhower signed off on a CIA document titled "A Program of Covert Action Against the Castro Regime." The CIA was tasked with undermining Castro's appeal through a disinformation campaign that was coupled with support for anti-communist dissidents in Cuba and Florida.

The program initially demonstrated little success, but when Kennedy was elected president, the CIA's anti-Castro program was given new life.

Kennedy gave the CIA a green light to move ahead with the Bay of Pigs invasion, and after that failure, they devised a much more intricate program to remove Castro through a series of plans and missions that became known as "Operation Mongoose."

Interestingly, as strange and cryptic as many of the names of some of these outlandish CIA missions were, the name "Operation Mongoose" was surprisingly logical. Communist Cuba was viewed as a snake by the CIA, and mongooses are small animals that kill snakes by attacking their heads, which was obviously equated with Castro.

Therefore, the goal of Operation Mongoose was to cause a regime change in Cuba without a major US military operation.

But as simple and straightforward as Operation Mongoose may have sounded to the military brass and CIA bigwigs, in reality, it proved to be much more difficult than advertised.

Castro was a crafty tinpot dictator, who had a loyal core of followers, commanded a capable intelligence network, and had the support of the USSR's KGB.

So, when CIA officer William King Harvey was given the lead on Operation Mongoose, he decided to employ tactics that were legally, ethically, and morally questionable, even for the CIA.

Before Operation Mongoose was official, Harvey employed American businessman Robert Maheu on one notable anti-Castro mission for the sake of "plausible deniability." Maheu ran a private detective agency that did "cut out" or subcontract work for the FBI and CIA when those organizations needed to circumvent the law.

Posing as a businessman with interests in Cuba, Maheu contacted Johnny Roselli of the Chicago Outfit Cosa Nostra organization with an offer to set up the assassination of Castro. Roselli liked the idea and organized a meeting between Maheu and Chicago Outfit boss Sam Giancana and Florida Mafia kingpin Santo Trafficante Junior in the early 1960s.

This would be the first - but far from the last - CIA attempt to assassinate Castro. After the Bay of Pigs failed, Operation Mongoose veered away from intelligence gathering and the overthrow of the regime generally to focus on assassinating Castro more specifically.

And over the nearly 50 years of Castro's rule, there would be some pretty incredible, and unbelievable, plots to kill him.

Exploding Cigars, Poison Pens, and TB

The CIA was desperate to get Castro, so much so that they seem to have employed science fiction writers to come up with some of the assassination methods.

Or maybe they were officers who were using some of the LSD from Project MKUltra?

Either way, it's almost unbelievable how crazy some of the ideas were.

The starting points of CIA's plans to kill Castro were soundly based on some of his weaknesses, but from there they seemed to devolve into the bizarre before they even got off the ground.

Take for instance Castro's love of scuba diving.

Being born and raised in the Caribbean, Castro loved the ocean and in his younger years was an avid scuba diver and snorkeler. He particularly enjoyed diving for mollusks, which is how the CIA came up with two of its early, failed plans to kill him.

The first involved CIA frogmen placing brightly-colored mollusks packed with explosives on the ocean floor where Castro routinely dove. When he would attempt to grab the explosive shell, he'd be sent to the worker's paradise in the sky where he could philosophize with the ghosts of Marx and Lenin.

When that plan didn't work for some reason, the CIA came up with the idea of infecting Castro's diving suit with a deadly fungus or toxin.

But officers just couldn't get close enough to do the deed.

And the CIA didn't really care if others got in the way of their plots or if a potential assassination happened in a neutral or even friendly country.

On November 22, 1963, the day that President Kennedy was assassinated (which may or may not be ironic), an anti-communist Cuban CIA operative named Nestor Sanchez met with a high-level Cuban military officer in Paris to give him the tools needed to kill Castro. The weapon wasn't a tool or a gun but a pen that contained a hypodermic needle filled with a deadly poison!

Castro was in Paris at the time, by some accounts meeting an American diplomat to discuss normalizing relations between the two countries. The potential assassin thought the operation was a suicide mission, so he suggested using a sniper rifle, and it was called off.

News of Kennedy's assassination may also have put a temporary damper on the plot to kill Castro, although more conspiracy-minded individuals believe it was supposed to be a double assassination that day.

But the CIA wouldn't be deterred. It had plenty of resources, officers, and crazy ideas left to try to kill the Cuban leader.

The CIA dipped into its MKUltra goodie bag for a variety of poisons and drugs it planned to use on Castro. Various schemes were set up to poison Castro's tea, coffee, and other drinks, but once again, the Agency had difficulties getting someone close enough to perform the task. The CIA even considered spraying an aerosol laced with LSD on Castro before he gave a speech. It was believed that the dose wouldn't have been fatal, but it may have made him look like a blabbering fool on television as he hallucinated.

Other crazy assassination plots reportedly focused on the things Castro loved most.

You may not believe this, but although Castro was a hardcore Marxist and hater of American "Yankee" imperialism, he loved the very American sport of baseball. Castro was said to be quite the player in his younger days and even considered attempting a professional career but instead opted to be a guerilla leader.

But even as Castro was fighting in the Sierra Maestra Mountains in the late 1950s, and after he became leader of Cuba, he continued his love of baseball.

The CIA used Castro's love of baseball against him when they sent assassins to kill him with grenades at a baseball game in Havana, but once more, the operation turned into a complete failure.

The CIA also tried to use almost any man's weakness against Castro - sex.

When Castro met one of his many mistresses, Marita Lopez, in 1959, little did he know that she was sent by the CIA to kill him? The details of how Lopez became involved with the CIA are sketchy but what is certain is that she had some poison pills in a cold cream jar that she planned to put in his food or drink.

But Castro became hip to the operation, probably after the pills melted and Lopez's demeanor changed as she tried to figure out what to do next. Castro decided for her, though, pulling out his pistol and handing it to her, challenging her to finish the job, which she couldn't.

Perhaps my favorite of all these failed CIA assassination plots involved Castro's favorite vice, and one of his most distinguishing trademarks, his love of cigars.

They say that Cuban cigars are the best in the world, and it's no secret that Castro loved cigars as much, if not more than baseball and women. So, when the dictator visited the United Nations in New York City in 1960, the CIA thought up the idea of giving him a lethal stogie.

Everyone loves a good exploding cigar gag, but the CIA planned to switch one of Castro's smooth Cubans for a cheap imitation laced with C4. Another potential plan was to lace one of his cigars with poison.

In the end, none of these crazy assassination attempts came close. Although there would be hundreds of attempts on Castro's life into the 2000s, most after Kennedy's assassination weren't sponsored by the CIA.

I guess the CIA decided Castro couldn't be killed so they moved on to other targets.

In the end, Castro had the last laugh. He died in 2016 at the age of 90, presumably of natural causes.

FROM CIA TO FEMINIST ICON

We've seen that the CIA has infiltrated a wide range of groups across the political spectrum and in doing so has created some pretty interesting situations and bedfellows. The Agency's infiltration of some of these groups has created a situation where many people have rightfully questioned its influence in some political groups.

Or even the *purpose* of some groups.

For instance, did the CIA infiltrate some of these groups to keep tabs on them? Or did the CIA do so to discredit them through scandals and false flag operations?

Is it possible the CIA infiltrated these groups with more complex, long-term goals in mind?

In some of these cases that have become public, it's hard to say for sure, such as that of feminist icon Gloria Steinem.

Gloria Steinem is known for her rabble-rousing, bra-burning, pro-feminist activism in the 1960s and '70s, which made her a celebrity and one of the most revered figures on the New Left.

But it was revealed in a 1979 article in the liberal *Village Voice* that Gloria Steinem had at one time worked as a CIA asset and that she very well may have still been one. The article certainly raised more than a few eyebrows with readers who had reasons to distrust the CIA.

Some thought it was slander and possibly disinformation *from* the CIA, while it made others question Steinem's entire life.

Steinem has, for the most part, avoided answering questions about her potential work with the CIA, but the fact remains that she rubbed elbows with known CIA officers and front groups during a period when the Agency had its hands in nearly every political organization in America. The obvious question then is if Steinem was working for the CIA, what was her mission?

An Unlikely Asset

The saying "it takes all types" is as true for CIA assets as it is for anything else. As the CIA has developed its vast network of leakers, snitches, and unofficial spies over the years, it's gone out of its way to make sure that people from all walks of life are represented.

All races.

Men and women.

All religions.

And all political persuasions.

And the CIA learned from its rival the KGB that there are plenty of ways to get a potential asset on board.

As we saw with Project MKUltra, sexual blackmail and outright drugging is one method.

Appeals to greed in the form of cash payouts and/or lucrative jobs have also been used.

Finally, the CIA has also appealed to many of its assets' patriotism or on ideological grounds, particularly anti-communism.

So, based on all of this, how feminist icon Gloria Steinem may have come to be a CIA asset may seem strange at first, but upon further examination, it makes plenty of sense.

Steinem was born in 1934 in Toledo, Ohio to a WASP mother and a Jewish father. Steinem's father was usually gone on business and her mother suffered from mental health problems. When Steinem's parents divorced when she was ten, she lived with her mother who had a difficult time making ends meet.

Steinem attributed this to sexism but dedicated herself to rise above what she saw as the proverbial "glass ceiling" by doing well in school and getting into a good college.

And when Steinem graduated from high school, she achieved that goal by being accepted to not just any school, but the prestigious, (at the time) women's school, Smith College. This is where Steinem's background gets interesting and where many people believe she was first recruited by the CIA.

Steinem did well in high school, but her family just didn't have the background or money for her to study at Smith. However, she was sharp and apparently had support from some influential people because not only did Steinem attend Smith College, she was also fast-tracked into a career among the elites.

After Steinem graduated from Smith in 1955, she was awarded a Chester Bowles Asian Fellow scholarship to study in India for two years, but examination of the scholarship's history reveals it to be something of a mystery.

The man who the scholarship is named after, and who presumably funded it, was Chester Bowles, a political liberal who believed in improving the developing world through loans and volunteerism. If you're wondering how someone like this could've been connected to the more conservative CIA of the Cold War Era, it's simply that the Cold War had its hands in all kinds of international aid organizations and NGOs at the time, and still presumably do.

Bowles may have been a liberal, but he believed in the American government and its potential to carry out some of his ideas, so he regularly rubbed shoulders with members of the CIA and other intelligence agencies.

So, when Gloria Steinem was awarded a fellowship in his name, it should be no surprise that she was possibly being groomed or "interviewed" for a more active role with the CIA. Curiously, Steinem is the only known recipient of the Chester Bowles Asian Fellow Scholarship.

Just who Steinem may have been communicating with while she was in India may never be known, nor if she was recruited by the CIA before accepting the fellowship. However, it isn't denied by anyone, including Steinem herself, that after she returned to the United States in 1958, she began actively working for the CIA.

In 1958, CIA officer Cord Meyer was running a CIA front group known as the Independent Research Service. The purpose of this organization was to bring together American academics, intellectuals, and journalists on the left-wing of the political spectrum, ostensibly to steer them away from communism and Marxism. Steinem in particular was tasked with helping send non-communist representatives to the World Festival of Youth and Students in Vienna, Austria in 1959.

The World Youth Festival was a semi-regular festival that was intended to show global youth and socialist solidarity. It was commonly held in communist nations, so the event in non-communist Austria in 1959 was a pretty big deal.

And I'm sure you're starting to see how the CIA saw it as an opportunity and - as crazy as it may sound - how Gloria Steinem could help them on that mission.

Steinem gave an interview in the late 1960s that was for the most part forgotten until the *Village Voice* article was published in the '70s. In the interview, Steinem admitted to being a CIA asset, claiming that there were no strings attached to the Agency's financial support for her participation in the 1959 World Youth Festival. She said:

"The private individuals to whom I went, often had particular points of view to put forward, which would have been much more restricting than the CIA funds, where they were free."

In the same interview, Steinem then described how the CIA was nothing at all what she thought it was, and that it was really just like the Peace Corps, stating:

"I had the conventional liberal's view of the CIA as a rightwing incendiary group, and I was amazed to discover that this was far from the case, that they were enlightened, liberal, non-partisan, activist sort who characterized the Kennedy administration, for instance."

In the same interview, Steinem claimed she hadn't worked for the CIA since 1962, going on to be a writer, editor, and full-time feminist activist. However, also in that same interview, she let something slip that exposed the confusing and duplicitous nature of the CIA and the crazy way in which they recruited people like her.

When asked if her work with the CIA hurt her street cred with the New Left, Steinem pointed out how she had protested the Vietnam War in front of Robert McNamara's office, who was Secretary of Defense from 1961 through 1968 and is largely seen as the architect of American involvement in Vietnam.

"This didn't precisely fit with the image of a CIA agent," Steinem said, but then continued with this curious point. "But then neither does the CIA."

The idea that Gloria Steinem was CIA asset seems crazy at first but isn't when you consider just how extensive CIA operations were in the 1950s and '60s. Steinem's acknowledgment that she worked for the CIA may be surprising to some, but in many ways, it only adds more confusion and questions to her background.

When did Steinem end her CIA involvement?

And even if Steinem quit officially working for the CIA, did she lose her security clearance?

Perhaps the biggest question, though, is why was Steinem recruited into the CIA in the first place?

Was she legitimately recruited because, as she and others claim, she was a young talented woman who happened to be at the right place at the right time to work for the CIA, which to her was little more than another version of the Peace Corps, complete with idealistic, liberal do-gooders running around with the sole intent to help the less fortunate?

The more cynical among you reading this, which is likely the majority, probably think Steinem was wound up and sent into the midst of the New Left to spy on some of the more radical and violent members. Steinem also may have served as effective "controlled opposition," whereby the CIA controlled dissident groups (Operation CHAOS) with their own officers.

We'll probably never know the extent of Gloria Steinem's involvement with the CIA, but it's pretty strange to think that the woman who led the second-wave feminist movement may have been reporting everything to a handler.

SPYING ON THE CHINESE FROM THE TOP OF THE WORLD

So far, most of the crazy CIA missions and colorful characters associated with the Agency profiled in this book have concerned the Soviet Union, its eastern European allies, and Cuba. But in 1949, when Mao Zedong took power, the sleeping giant - or dragon - of China suddenly became the world's most populous communist nation.

The situation threw the US government and the CIA into a tailspin. It seemed to be another victory for the communist forces in the Cold War, which was something the crew at Langley weren't going to take lightly.

But the reality is, no one really knew what to do with China, and that includes the Soviets.

Yes, Mao had proclaimed China to be a socialist/communist state, but the more reports that leaked out of China in the 1950s, the less it looked like anything people could understand. It was clearly a dictatorship that claimed to be communist, but in many ways, it looked more like some ancient peasant society than the Soviet Union.

At first, the US kept communist China at an arm's length, but then the Korean War (1950-1952) took place, which put China and the US in direct conflict.

That war ended in a stalemate, and although China was clearly still a backward country whose army was undersupplied, their sheer numbers were enough to frighten everyone in the American military-industrial complex.

The only thing the Chinese were missing were nukes, but by the mid-1960s, they were on the verge of getting those too.

The government tasked the CIA with spying on the Chinese nuclear program, and what followed was one of the Agency's strangest uses of technology: a listening device placed on one of the highest peaks in the world - which failed to be of any use to the government.

Building the Bomb

In 1954, the only things China and the Soviet Union/Russia had in common were their supposed commitments to Marxism/socialism/communism and their practice of totalitarian government. The Russians and Chinese didn't have much in common culturally and through much of the course of their long histories, they weren't really in contact.

Contact between Russia and China became more common in the 1700s, however, and by the late 1800s, Russia was the stronger of the two nations and had even opened ports and settlements in China.

By the time Mao unified China under his rule, though, things had changed again and the border region became a bit contentious.

Still, the Soviets agreed to lend materials, technology, and scientists to make a bomb to their communist counterparts.

Or several bombs.

Actually, Mao wasn't very greedy. He just wanted enough bombs to use as a threat to keep his country from being invaded by the Yankee imperialist Americans. But in an ironic twist of geopolitics, after 1959, China's new nuclear arsenal was more likely to be used on the Soviet Union or India.

Mao claimed that the Soviets weren't being communist enough, so in 1959, he made it known to the world that he and the Chinese Communist Party would go their own way and any socialist nations in good standing were free to join them.

And they were taking their bombs with them!

Things Don't Always Go as Planned

The US government found itself in a bit of an intelligence pickle when the Chinese government performed its first nuclear weapons test in 1964. The pace with which the Chinese went from being a nearly completely agrarian society to nuclear power was impressive, to say the least - a little *too* impressive for the Americans and the Indians.

As much as the Americans wanted to keep tabs on all other nuclear powers, especially those professing undying loyalty to communism, the Indians didn't want to see Chinese power grow either. China and India had their own border conflict over the Himalaya Mountains region, so when the Chinese got the bomb, it put a sense of urgency into the Indian Intelligence Bureau (IB), which is India's version of the CIA.

86

So, the CIA and IB decided to collaborate on a mission to spy on China's burgeoning nuclear weapons program.

But how were they going to accomplish this task?

It's not that the two agencies couldn't effectively cooperate - they did - but obtaining intelligence became the major hurdle.

What about the tried-and-true method of using officers in the field?

Well, this sort of thing worked in the USSR for a number of reasons. Despite technically being a closed society, the USSR did allow a sizable number of outsiders to visit and sometimes even work and live in the country. Most of the USSR was also in Europe, so the people had a long tradition of being part of Europe and had, by the 1960s, developed ties across the continent that transcended the Iron Curtain.

But in the 1960s, China was a truly closed and very foreign country.

It would've been difficult to send Chinese American spies into China and attempting to turn Chinese citizens was seen as a futile exercise.

So, if sending officers into China wasn't a possibility in 1965, what about spy satellites?

Spy satellites work great, but the technology just wasn't there in the mid-1960s. Remember, the Space Race itself between the Soviet Union and the US was less than ten years old, which meant that the CIA had to look elsewhere.

"Hmmm, okay, well what about all those big mountains in the Himalayas?

The CIA came up with the idea of placing a listening device on a Himalayan mountain that was close enough to the Chinese border and high enough to intercept Chinese radio signals. After doing some investigating, the CIA came up with a mountain called Nanda Devi as the location for their device.

This was how Operation Hat was born.

Named after a Hindu goddess, Nanda Devi rises 25,646 feet high, demonstrating her majesty over the region. Nanda Devi is the 23rd highest mountain in the world, but when it comes to access, it's among the most difficult to scale.

Unlike the better-known Mount Everest, Nanda Devi is much more isolated and its summit was only first reached by climbers in 1936. Since that time, very few climbers have attempted to climb Nanda Devi's summit, but in 1965, a team of American and Indian climbers was assembled by the CIA and IB to place a top-secret listening device on the mountain.

And as extraordinary as the mission was to place the device, the device itself was truly out of this world.

Since Nanda Devi is so isolated, and because the listening device had to be placed in a cold crevice on the mountain, it couldn't be a standard radio receiver. The only way the CIA could get a receiver on the mountain that could pick up the Chinese broadcasts *and* be durable enough for the long-term was to equip it with its own power source.

So, how did they do that?

Well, nuclear power, of course.

I guess since the CIA was spying on China's nuclear weapons program, it was apropos that they used nuclear power to undertake this mission. The listening device weighed about 123 pounds and was powered by 11 pounds of plutonium, which could be a real mess if it leaked.

But what did that matter to the CIA? They reasoned no one lived anywhere near Nanda Devi so it posed little risk to anyone. That may be the case but placing the device and maintaining it was apparently more of a task than the CIA considered.

Since spies aren't known for their mountain-climbing skills, the CIA and IB had to compile their team primarily from civilians with mountain-climbing experience.

Once assembled, the team was given a crash course on intelligence and flown to Mount McKinley, Alaska in the summer of 1965 to begin training. All team members were expert climbers, but most knew little about how to handle the potentially deadly plutonium rods that would power the listening device.

The team arrived in India in October 1965, and after preparing at a base camp for a couple of weeks, they began their long ascent to the summit of Nanda Devi. It was far from easy, considering that winter was approaching and the climbers were burdened with carrying such a large, potentially dangerous piece of equipment.

As the team got 2,000 feet from the summit (that may not seem like much, but when you're already more than 20,000 above sea level, inches can seem like miles), a storm kicked up, forcing them to descend. They left the device where they were, with plans to return in the spring of 1965 to finish the job.

This is where this unique and slightly strange CIA mission begins veering into strange territory.

When the team returned in the spring, they made their arduous journey back to where the nuclear-powered listening device had been left...but they didn't find anything except for some rocks and snow. The team searched in vain for the device and after a while, had to return to the basecamp to report the situation to their CIA and IB handlers.

Up until this point, the mission had been pretty straightforward, but if you've read the book this far, you should know that when it comes to CIA missions, especially the ones profiled in this book, *nothing* is straightforward.

The CIA had no idea what happened to their precious device. The most logical explanation was that it had been buried in an avalanche. However, there were rumors that the Pakistanis had somehow found out about the plan and gone up there to retrieve the device to provide the core of their own nuclear weapons program.

Others think the Chinese may have gotten wind of the operation and taken it.

But the more cynical think the Indians actually took the device and placed it somewhere else so they wouldn't have to share intelligence with the Americans.

Or maybe it was Nanda Devi herself enacting revenge for disturbing her sacred mountain. With the absence of any hard evidence, it's as good an explanation as any other.

As crazy as the circumstances surrounding the disappearance of the device on Nanda Devi may have been, the CIA is nothing if not persistent, so they organized another expedition.

A Nuclear Meltdown

In 1967, Operation Hat was put into effect once again, but this time the American Indian team climbed Nanda Kot, which although in the Himalayas was thought to be a bit more accessible than Nanda Devi. The team made it to the summit of the mountain, more than 22,500 feet high, and they placed a new nuclear-powered listening device and flipped the "on" switch.

The second device actually worked!

Well, it worked for a while anyway, about one year.

When the device quit transmitting signals, another team was sent to Nanda Kat to see what had happened.

They were surprised and a bit horrified by what they found.

The nuclear-powered transmitter had generated so much power, and heat, that it had melted eight feet into the side of the mountain! This was just another consequence the CIA hadn't thought of (that seems to be a theme with the CIA, doesn't it?), so the decision was made to shut down the operation. The device was removed from the mountain and no more nuclear-powered listening devices were ever used.

Or, at least, that we know of.

By the late 1960s, technology had developed enough that spy satellites would be a reality within a few years. Also, China opened up enough in the 1970s that assets were able to be placed.

The CIA would probably like to forget its failed attempts to listen to the Chinese from the top of the world with nuclear-powered devices, but fortunately, the crazy mission known as Operation Hat is part of the world's historical record.

CIA BLOWUP DOLLS

So far, we've looked at some truly bizarre CIA missions and projects. Some have been extremely strange, while others have been extremely violent. This next project can only be described as extremely funny.

Yes, it seems that the team at the CIA maybe did have a sense of humor in the 1970s, or maybe they were just so square they didn't see the humor in this project.

Or maybe they took some of the leftover MKUltra LSD stash!

Whatever it was, it's hard to keep a straight face when you read about the CIA's use of blowup dolls in the 1970s and '80s. In case you're wondering, yes, I do mean the anatomically correct, life-size plastic dolls that lonely people use for...

This crazy project was at least partly the brainchild of a CIA asset we've already met - John Chambers - along with some other officers, who I like to believe had a sense of humor to go along with their cloak and dagger operations.

Keeping It Real

To understand why the CIA thought using blow-up dolls was a good idea, or how it was actually done, a little background on the espionage world of the 1970s is needed. It was mentioned earlier that the KGB had a head start on the CIA, and although the CIA and other American intelligence agencies had scored some notable victories, by the '70s, they were routinely getting their butts kicked in the espionage field.

A big part of this had to do with the differences in American and Soviet society at the time.

The US was a more or less open country that allowed and even encouraged foreign tourists and immigrants to visit and stay, while the Soviet Union, on the other hand, was much more restrictive. Foreigners were allowed to visit the USSR and some even immigrated there, but you can be sure that if you were a foreigner in the Soviet Union during the Cold War, you were being watched.

Then there was the difference in the economies.

America's love of capitalism invites greed and not far behind greed is corruption. KGB officers who freely roamed the US often appealed to Americans' greed to get them to turn over valuable intelligence. On the other hand, since the Soviet Union tightly controlled its people's bank accounts, and there were few luxury items available anyway, CIA officers weren't as successful in using greed to turn Soviet citizens.

Finally, the Soviets had a culture that supported the KGB more than the Americans did the CIA.

The KGB wasn't hampered with pesky things like constitutions, civil rights, and lawyers who specialized in those things, and it also enjoyed nearly unlimited funding from the Soviet government. Although we've seen how the CIA did pretty much what it wanted outside the US, it was technically restrained by laws and American public opinion has always been a bit capricious toward the agency.

All of this meant that the KGB usually had the advantage over the CIA, especially in the Soviet Union. CIA officers working in the Soviet Union (usually under a diplomatic passport) were constantly followed by the KGB so they had to work extra hard to turn assets. Even when they did turn one, they had to devise some clever ways to meet them.

Dead drops only work to an extent; sometimes, an officer has to meet their asset in person. For those cases, the CIA turned to Walter McIntosh, the head of the CIA's disguise unit from 1977 to 1979.

McIntosh was told that he needed to create a dummy - or something that looked like a person - that CIA officers could leave in their cars while meeting with their Russian informants on the cold streets of Moscow. Although KGB officers tailed CIA officers constantly in the Soviet Union, the Soviet spies made sure never to get too close to their targets. The distance gave the Americans just enough time to get out of their car, quickly meet the informant, and then get back.

But they needed a dummy or something that looked like a person from a distance to be in the car while the meeting took place.

McIntosh knew that carrying a complete dummy around in a car on the streets of Moscow would be impractical, so he looked for something a bit smaller and more disposable.

After doing some brainstorming and searching, McIntosh found what he was looking for while researching a porno shop in Washington, D.C. Or, at least, McIntosh *said* he was doing research when he noticed that blow-up sex dolls may have been the answer the CIA was looking for.

As McIntosh began developing his first doll, he knew he had to make it look real. So, to keep it real, so he consulted with two well-known Hollywood makeup artists - John Chambers and Les Smith. We've already seen how Chambers went from Hollywood to Langley, and Smith's journey to CIA asset was quite similar.

Smith owned a makeup and magic store in southern California in the 1970s and frequently worked on films and TV shows. He was a friend and colleague of Chambers, who introduced him to McIntosh and the CIA lifestyle.

The two men consulted with McIntosh to keep any mission that used one of their dolls as real as possible. It only needed to look real from a distance because chances are no KGB officer would get too close. Also, CIA officers in the Soviet Union usually worked in pairs, so the officer in the passenger side of the car was usually the one who met with the asset.

McIntosh knew that the doll had to be quickly revealed during meetings to not arouse suspicion with the prying eyes of the KGB. So, he came up with a device he called the "Jack in the Box" or JIB.

The JIB was simply a modified blow-up doll in a modified briefcase. When the CIA officer ran from the passenger side of the car to meet with his informant, he opened the briefcase and up popped Jack!

Well, it was supposed to work that way. When CIA officers had an urgent meeting with one of their sources in Moscow planned in December 1982, they decided to put the JIB into operation.

The CIA desperately needed to meet with one of their top Moscow sources whom they hadn't heard from for a while. Two CIA officers zigged and zagged around Moscow until they found a blind spot where the officer in the passenger seat could jump out and meet the source on foot. As he leapt from the car, he activated the JIB, which was in a birthday cake, of all things.

It was a success. The KGB officers apparently didn't suspect a thing.

The JIB continued to be used by CIA officers in the Soviet Union, but its most notable use came in 1985 in the US.

Defecting with the JIB

In 1985, Edward Lee Howard was a 34-year-old CIA washout who had been spying for the Soviets for the last two years. The walls were closing in on the booze-addled traitor when he made his big move to defect to the Soviets.

And he did so, using a JIB.

Howard was an unimpressive man with an alcohol problem when he began working for the CIA in 1980. Before that time, Howard had worked for aid organizations and environmental groups; not the dyed in the wool conservative you'd think would be drawn to the CIA, but as Gloria Steinem said, the CIA isn't always as it seems.

Howard began his CIA career in counterintelligence and learned all the tricks of the CIA, otherwise known as "tradecraft." One of the primary tradecrafts Howard learned was the JIB, which he would probably use when he was assigned to Moscow in 1983. Before he could take the big promotion, though, he just had to pass a polygraph test.

Polygraph tests aren't exactly "lie detector tests," as they're often called, and only really gauge the subject's reactions to certain questions and their stress levels more than anything. You can "beat" a polygraph exam by remaining calm, as notorious American spy Aldrich Ames proved in the early 1990s.

But Edward Howard was no Aldrich Ames when it came to espionage.

Howard's exam came back showing "deception" on questions about his past drug use, and when combined with his current alcohol abuse, this led to the Agency firing him in 1983.

The CIA may have burned Howard, but Howard had enough material to burn them and several officers in return.

Angered at his perceived poor treatment by the CIA, Howard vowed revenge and began spilling his guts to the KGB about all the CIA's dirty little secrets in Moscow.

The CIA and FBI eventually learned from one of their Soviet assets that Howard had turned traitor, so they moved in to arrest him in New Mexico in 1985. However, the disgraced officer had one last trick up his sleeve.

As his wife was driving them home from dinner, Howard noticed they were being tailed. When they turned around a corner, Howard leapt from the car and his wife opened a JIB that was on the passenger seat.

Howard was able to flee from the country and defect to the Soviet Union, where he lived the rest of his life.

CIA blow-up dolls had an interesting and crazy life. They proved to be quite useful in ways the original manufacturers probably never envisioned. Howard's use of a JIB to escape

97

from American spooks is the last notable time one was used in espionage…or was it?

Who knows? Don't be surprised if, in 20 years, we read about a different way the CIA used blow-up dolls to gather intelligence. You can use your imagination…

Or not!

DID YOU KNOW?

- It is estimated that the CIA attempted to kill Fidel Castro 638 times, which doesn't include several more attempted hits by freelance Cuban ex-pats. The numerous attempts on the dictator's life were chronicled in a 2006 British Broadcasting Company documentary, *638 Ways to Kill Castro*.

- The nuclear meltdown on Nanda Kot proved to be a meltdown in other ways for the Indians as well. The CIA and IB obviously wanted to keep their Himalayan failures a secret for as long as possible, but the word of the meltdown on Nanda Kot hit the Indian news media in 1978. The Indian public wasn't happy with the situation, although many were willing to overlook it as they saw the Chinese as a threat to their country.

- An interesting postscript to the life of Edward Howard is how he lived and died after he defected to the Soviet Union. Howard apparently lived a good life, as he had a dacha (Soviet summer home) in the country, which is where he died in 2002, breaking his neck falling from a horse. Hmmm, do you really think it was a horse that broke his neck?

- One of the silliest proposed plans within Operation Mongoose was to poison Fidel Castro with thallium salts.

The plan called for lacing his shoes with the chemical when he left them out to be cleaned at the hotel he was staying at in New York. It was believed that after he touched his shoes, the thallium poisoning would make his beard fall out, causing him to somehow be discredited. Yes, this plan was actually floated by seasoned espionage agents!

- The operation to storm Osama bin Laden's compound was known as Operation Neptune Spear for the trident that appears on the Navy SEAL's insignia. It was never clear if the objective was to kill or capture bin Laden. Former CIA director Leon Panetta said that if bin Laden attempted to surrender, they would've taken him alive, but military officials claimed it was a search and destroy mission.

THE FIRST EARTH BATTALION, REMOTE VIEWING, AND OTHER CIA PARANORMAL EXPERIMENTS

When Joseph Stalin was running the Soviet Union from 1922 until he died in 1953, he embarked on some pretty ambitious programs. He forcibly incorporated the Baltic states and Ukraine into the Soviet Union, initiated "five-year plans" to rapidly industrialize the country, and collectivized the farms. Some of his policies did indeed modernize the Soviet Union, but many led to the deaths of millions of people.

But perhaps Stalin's most ambitious program is also his most overlooked: experiments in parapsychology.

Almost as soon as Stalin came to power, he ordered scientists to study paranormal phenomena such as telepathy, remote viewing, precognition, invisibility, and just about anything relating to mental powers you can think of. For years, most people didn't know that the Soviets were conducting these experiments, but thanks to some spies, word of them began leaking out to the West in the 1960s and '70s.

Not wanting to be outdone by what could possibly be an incredible weapon - the human mind - the CIA and the

American military eventually began conducting their own experiments into extra-sensory perception (ESP).

You may have seen the 2009 film *The Men Who Stare at Goats*, starring George Clooney. Or maybe you remember the 1984 film *Firestarter*, starring a young Drew Barrymore, which was based on the Stephen King book of the same name? Both books turned movies deal with the subject of the CIA and the military doing some pretty bizarre experiments in ESP, but as wild as those films are, they are based on *some* facts.

The true story of the CIA's use of ESP may not be as scary as *Firestarter* or as funny as *The Men Who Stare at Goats*, but it is a story worth telling and it's guaranteed to make you scratch your head and question some of the things you've taken for granted.

The First Earth Battalion

In the late 1970s, Jim Channon was a career officer in the US Army who had served two combat tours with the infantry in Vietnam. Channon had seen plenty of action and experienced all the horrors of war, so when he returned to the States, like many men who've seen combat, he was a changed man. While still on active duty with the Army in the late 1970s, he traveled among hippy communes in California.

It was at this point that Channon was probably working for Army Intelligence, the CIA, or both because when he reemerged in 1979, he was at the center of a bizarre plan to create hippy super soldiers.

Yes, hippy super soldiers!

If you've seen *The Men Who Stare at Goats* then you probably remember the eccentric character played by Jeff Bridges. The character was based somewhat loosely on the real-life Jim Channon. Channon was every bit as eccentric as the character in the movie, and in 1982, he published a manual titled *First Earth Battalion Guidelines*.

Channon called those in his unit "warrior monks" and as he wrote in the manual, they would serve a higher ideal for the world, not just the United States.

"I envision an international ideal of service awakening in an emerging class of people who are best called evolutionaries," he wrote. *"I see them as soldiers, as youth, and as those who have soldier spirit within them."*

The manual is full of Channon's hippy philosophy, but it also relates how technology and drugs (hello MKUltra?) can be used to create these warrior monks and change the world.

Channon retired from the military in 1983 and apparently took the First Earth Battalion with him, but the eccentric Army officer influenced several later ESP experiments by the military and the CIA.

Remote Viewing and ESP

Although the First Earth Battalion failed to produce a cadre of super soldiers for the military, it opened the doors for the CIA to indulge its fascination with the strange in the form of the Stargate Project.

Yes, that was the name of a real CIA-US Military joint project and not just the name of a sci-fi film and TV series.

As interest in the paranormal increased and the US government learned of the Stalin era paranormal experiments, the Defense Intelligence Agency (DIA) (the US military's version of the CIA) teamed up with the CIA to create their own experiments. This was partially how the First Earth Battalion was formed, but the DIA-CIA experiments, collectively known as the Stargate Project, went beyond the esoteric ramblings of a drop-out Army officer by focusing on remote viewing and other observable psychic phenomena.

Remote viewing is the process whereby a person with presumably psychic abilities can view people, places, or things hundreds or even thousands of miles away. Of course, the military and CIA believed that anyone with this ability could help them learn more about the Soviets and other enemies of the USA, so they began assembling as many psychics as they could in the early 1970s to conduct the project.

Some real "interesting" types came on board.

The CIA and DIA funded the studies of Hal Putoff, a Scientologist who claimed his knowledge of the pseudo-religion of Scientology gave him the ability to remote view. Putoff then brought on board people like the Israeli illusionist Uri Geller who became famous for "bending" spoons with his mind on live television.

Although Geller's lack of psychic abilities was seemingly exposed by talk show host Johnny Carson in 1973 on *The Tonight Show with Johnny Carson*, the Stargate Project continued to fund him.

Ingo Swann was another interesting character who worked on the Stargate Project. Swann's claim to fame was as a remote viewing "expert" who always did well in experiments he controlled but not so well in those controlled by others.

The Stargate Project was completely turned over to the CIA in 1995. They then shut it down, claiming that it was basically a failure.

But were the CIA claims completely truthful?

Declassified documents show some of the Stargate Project experiments actually were successful. Based on that, some claim the CIA still uses psychics in some of their missions.

Despite claiming that the Stargate Project was a failure, there are cases where the CIA claims subjects did correctly identify some objects remotely. In one particular test, CIA officers would put pictures and words in sealed envelopes and have the test subjects guess what was in them. In the overwhelming number of cases, the subjects failed, but in a few cases, they guessed correctly, again and again.

Those who performed well on the tests were then given more difficult tests, such as sending messages to each other from different buildings using only their minds. Officers working on these projects claim that the tests were occasionally successful and that some subjects demonstrated what appeared to be amazing psychic abilities.

Then there was the psychic who described the apocalypse on Mars.

In a 1984 remote viewing experiment, CIA officers decided to throw a real curveball to a supposed psychic when they wrote the name of a location on a card and asked the subject to describe it. Instead of writing the Amazon River, Paris, or some other well-known place, they wrote "The Planet Mars: 1 million BC."

According to a declassified report, the psychic described strange-looking people who lived in an advanced society with plenty of pyramid-like buildings. Their society was dying so they "sent out" explorers to find a new place to live, but they could only wait and die.

The experiment doesn't prove life ever existed on Mars, or that the experiment was successful in any way, but it certainly is creepy and a bit bizarre. It also shows that there was probably a bit more to the Stargate Project than the CIA is willing to admit.

In addition to researching remote viewing, the CIA has also reportedly used police psychics to find missing persons and during hostage crises.

So, if you can move things with your mind, see through walls, or levitate, get a hold of the CIA (somehow) because they may be hiring!

GRASS ROOTS POLITICAL MOVEMENTS OR CIA OPERATIONS?

We've seen how during the Cold War the CIA influenced and corrupted foreign (and the US?) governments, and we'll look at one particularly crazy example of this a little later. The US government, its allies, and even the American people gave the CIA wide latitude to do some pretty crazy things because they were fighting communism. No matter what kind of wacky thing the CIA may have done back in those days, most people were willing to look the other way.

If the CIA was overthrowing a foreign government, there was a good reason for it, or so most people thought. Besides, that all ended with the Cold War, right?

The end of the Cold War didn't mean that world peace was upon us, and it surely didn't signal the "end of history" as political scientist Francis Fukuyama argued. No, geopolitics just changed and some would argue the world got even more dangerous.

The 9-11 attacks happened in the post-Cold War world, as did the Madrid train bombings, and the 7-7 attacks in London.

In fact, in 2020 the *Bulletin of Atomic Scientists* put the Doomsday Clock at just over one minute to midnight (midnight is doomsday on their hypothetical clock), which is the closest it's ever been.

So, with all this instability in the post-Cold War world, it shouldn't come as a surprise that there have actually been quite a few revolutions, on just about every continent. These revolutions have all had similar features. The governments are ruled by older men who many perceive to be autocrats, while the protesters/revolutionaries tend to be young people who take to the streets, almost always supported by Western media.

These revolutions have become known as "color revolutions" and many people around the world believe that it's more than just the media in the West who support them. The Russian and Chinese governments as well as some intellectuals and writers in the West have accused the CIA and other Western intelligence agencies of playing an active role in these color revolutions. If true, it would be perhaps the CIA's most wide-ranging and craziest operation yet.

It would involve millions of people, countless dollars, and affect the course of world history for decades or more to come.

For the most part, the CIA has remained mum on color revolutions, neither affirming nor denying participation. However, there is plenty of anecdotal evidence that points to it at least playing a peripheral role in some anti-government protests.

So, let's take a look at what color revolutions are and a few of the more notable ones so you can decide if these are the most outlandish CIA missions of all.

Revolution Is Fun!

Revolutions have existed since the beginning of human civilization in one form or another. In pre-modern cultures, they usually took the form of palace coups where a king or emperor would be forcefully removed from power, and usually beheaded, and then a regime change would take place...that affected most of the population very little. In the strictest sense of the definition, some would call these coup d'états and not revolutions, but for the sake of our discussion, we're talking about the overthrow of a government from *within* a society.

Things started to change in the 1500s and 1600s when peasant revolts and civil war became more common in Europe, and then all hell broke loose in the 1700s.

The American Revolution and the French Revolution, both in the 1700s, were two of the most important revolutions in world history, and along with the Bolshevik Revolution in Russia in 1917-1918, they represent the "trifecta" of modern revolutions.

But the reality is that those revolutions were all led by middle-aged men.

Whether it was in America, France, or Russia, the revolutionaries of those earlier eras were all men with worldly experience, and many had their own families. That all changed after World War II.

Once the dust and the haze of the war settled and people began rebuilding, the baby boom took place, and by the 1960s, things had changed considerably. Political demonstrations, revolutions, and even guerilla insurgencies became more common. We've seen how the CIA had their hand in much of this, but so did the

KGB and other intelligence agencies from around the world. The intelligence agencies may have been pulling the levers, but the people on the streets were usually young adults.

By the late '60s, revolution suddenly became hip and cool.

The Hungarian Revolution of 1956 was the first attempted anti-communist revolution in the world, and although it failed, it provided a template for future revolts and something the CIA could work with. It was primarily led by young men and although it turned quite violent, it started with mostly peaceful protests.

The People Power or Yellow Revolution in the Philippines in 1986 is often seen as the first of the color revolutions. Dictator Ferdinand Marcos was removed from power in this mostly peaceful revolution that was led by youth street protests. Then, in late 1989, the Velvet Revolution ended Communist rule in Czechoslovakia, led to the partition of that country, and marked the beginning of the end of communism in eastern Europe.

The Velvet Revolution was led by younger Czechs and Slovaks, male and female, in peaceful street protests, which some say were supported by intelligence services. Some people have alleged the KGB led the Velvet Revolution to give the collapse of communism a "soft landing," while others say the CIA and Western intelligence agencies had a hand in it.

Once communism collapsed in Europe, the color revolutions picked up steam and began spreading around the world.

If you can find one point where non-profit organizations/NGOs, Color Revolutions, and the CIA came together, it was a rather nondescript man named Gene Sharp. Sharp received his PhD in political theory from Oxford University in 1968 and then went on to teach at elite universities such as Harvard and Dartmouth. He worked for several non-profit organisations which had CIA, state department, and Pentagon connections including the RAND Corporation, the National Endowment for Democracy, and the Ford Foundation.

Books and articles written by Sharp have been cited as being the ideological and methodological framework for many Color Revolutions, such as the 2011 Lotus Revolution that removed dictator Hosni Mubarak from power and the 2004 Orange Revolution in Ukraine.

Most of these color revolutions actually failed, but the Orange Revolution was probably the most successful and ultimately was where the CIA was most involved.

Moving Closer to the West

The Orange Revolution in Ukraine began when pro-Russian politician Victor Yanukovych took the lead in the second round of voting in the 2004 presidential election. Accusations of corruption led to youth street protests and pro-Western candidate Viktor Yushchenko being declared the winner.

Yanukovych would later win the presidency in 2010, though, and initiated a pro-Russian geopolitical position.

Pro-Western elements in Ukraine didn't like the situation, but Western intelligence agencies liked it even less. Although the Cold War was over, Russia was still considered an enemy by most of the leaders of the West. The KGB may have changed its name to the FSB, but it was still playing the same cloak and dagger games with the CIA.

The big turn came when youth street protests, known as the "Euromaiden Protests," took place in Kiev's Euro Square in November 2013. The protesters said they were standing up to human rights abuses by the government, but the more cynical observers pointed out that the president had suspended Ukraine's decision to join the European Union.

Yanukovych wanted to keep Ukraine in the Russian political sphere.

The peaceful Euromaiden protests turned to violence in February 2014. A bizarre coalition of neo-Nazis and leftists who were pro-Western fought battles in the streets against pro-government, pro-Russian forces who came from equally opposing sides of the political spectrum.

It was clear to most that intelligence agencies were supporting factions on both sides.

When the smoke cleared, the pro-Western forces had won. Yanukovych went into exile in Russia and the new Ukrainian government was firmly pro-Western, promptly joining the EU and NATO.

Ukraine may have been the most successful color revolution, long-term, but 2011 was the year of the color revolution. As noted earlier, Mubarak was overthrown that year, and color revolutions were also attempted, but failed, in Syria, Russia, and China.

More recently, political protests in Cuba have been suggested to be the start of a color revolution in that country. They exhibit all the hallmarks: youth-led street protests opposed to an autocratic government. And with the history of CIA involvement in Cuba, it would be quite naïve to think the Agency didn't have officers and assets on the ground in Havana.

So, that leaves us with our original question: are color revolutions legitimate youth protests, or are they carefully orchestrated CIA operations? It's undeniable that the CIA had a hand in at least some of these protests, with the most solid evidence coming from Ukraine, but it's also difficult to say it was involved in every color revolution.

One thing is for sure: Gene Sharp wasn't the only political theorist with ties to non-profits with endless sources of revenue *and* the CIA. There's a good chance that in addition to whatever's happening in Cuba, the CIA might just be planning the next apple, mango, or banana revolution right now — and that's pretty bizarre!

CIA PORN

So, we know that the CIA has had a pretty cozy relationship with Hollywood over the years. We've seen how Hollywood types like John Chambers worked for the CIA, and the Agency's influence in film and television has likely been much deeper than most people realize. In fact, some well-known movies and TV shows were probably produced, written, and directed by CIA assets.

But has the CIA ever *directly* made a movie?

Well, we don't know for sure if the CIA had a direct hand in either version of *The Manchurian Candidate*, or how much influence its members had in the creation of the 'Jack Ryan' or 'Jason Bourne' characters, but we *do* know the CIA produced a porno film and considered making others.

That's right, the CIA made a hardcore porn film in the 1960s, then made a softcore film in the 2000s, and considered further productions. The films were made to discredit leaders, but they were so terrible that the CIA bigshots realized they wouldn't have the desired effect.

So, why did the CIA get into the porn business?

Who "starred" in these lurid "films"?

And why did the CIA finally pull the plug after producing them?

Sukarno and Sexual Blackmail

The CIA's foray into smut began in 1959 when the president and prime minister of Indonesia - the eponymously named Sukarno - began leading his country on a path that the CIA and many in the US government didn't like. Sukarno hung out with plenty of communists, and despite claiming to be a nationalist, he accepted many of their ideas when he led Indonesia in the years after it obtained independence from the Netherlands following World War II.

But thanks to colonialism, Sukarno found himself in a tough position.

The nation of Indonesia didn't exist before the Dutch ruled that part of the world, and after it became a nation-state, it found itself in a curious position. Although in east Asia Buddhism is the most popular religion, most of Indonesia's population is Muslim, with significant minorities of Buddhists, Christians, and the province of Bali is predominantly Hindu. In addition to the religious diversity, there are more than 1,300 ethnic groups and more than 700 languages spoken in Indonesia.

As you can imagine, when Indonesia attained independence, there were just as many political parties as there were ethnic and religious groups, but the largest tended to be the communists, Islamists, and nationalists.

So, Sukarno had to carefully navigate all these groups who lived on the thousands of islands of this archipelago nation.

Sukarno was well respected by Indonesians of all backgrounds due to his ability to bring people together and how he stood up to the Dutch, an act that had earned him a prison sentence as a revolutionary.

Things got tougher for Sukarno and Indonesia after he was released, as Japan conquered the country, along with most of Asia, putting it under its heel during World War II.

After the war, when Indonesia attained its complete independence, Sukarno had the unenviable task of bringing all those political factions, ethnic groups, and religions together under one government. He was able to do so with some authoritarian control he called "guided democracy."

Sukarno carried out economic reforms that were socialist and even worse, at least as far as the CIA was concerned, he began buddying up with a few of America's enemies at the time. Although Indonesia never declared itself a communist state, and it never became a BFF of the Soviet Union, it did get close to the so-called "Non-Aligned States."

During the Cold War, the Non-Aligned States were the countries that were not in the NATO or Warsaw Pact alliances. Led initially by India, many of these countries were communist, such as Cuba and Yugoslavia, while others, such as Egypt, had one foot in the Islamic world and the other in the socialist world.

Indonesia was in a similar position to Egypt and the CIA didn't like it.

Already by the early 1960s, US military "advisors" and CIA officers were in Vietnam. To President Kennedy, it seemed as though Indonesia could slip into the communist grip at any time.

After all, Sukarno was involved in territorial disputes with the Netherlands, he was hanging out with communists in Indonesia and around the world, and he had "nationalized" several large foreign companies.

The last point was probably the most important in some ways. When Western companies saw their assets seized by Sukarno in a nationalization campaign in the early 1960s, they put immense pressure on Western governments to do something about it. The governments then looked to the trusty CIA to come up with a solution.

The CIA's solution was to make a porno movie!

The CIA was actually supporting right-wing insurgency groups in Indonesia, but due to a lack of popular support and the fractured geographical nature of the country, revolution proved to be ineffective.

Blackmail also didn't work, so then the CIA decided to do the next best thing and make it *look* like Sukarno was doing something wrong.

Since it was the 1960s and the CIA was experimenting plenty with drugs and sex, the CIA decided that they would make a porno starring some guy who looked like Sukarno.

The CIA called their film *Happy Days* (It had nothing to do with Richie and Fonzie), and the premise was supposed to be that Sukarno had somehow been secretly filmed having a romp in the hay. The idea was that it would discredit him in the patriarchal, socially conservative, and predominantly Muslim nation. The CIA reasoned he would be viewed as a philanderer and adulterer who was dumb enough to get caught cheating on his wife, on film.

The CIA actually produced the porno, although many of the details remain a mystery. It's unknown who the actors were, how much they were paid, or even if a copy still exists. What is known about *Happy Days*, though, is that it was never released in Indonesia, or anywhere else.

Unbelievably, the idea of a porno to discredit a CIA enemy continued in the minds of officers and was given serious consideration again in the 2000s.

Saddam Hussein and Osama bin Laden Were Gay?

Well, no, or at least not that we know, but the CIA did apparently float the idea of making them look that way in CIA-produced porn.

The idea first surfaced before the US-led invasion of Iraq in 2003. As the War on Terror kicked into high gear after the 9-11 attacks, the American intelligence and military-industrial complexes set their targets on several enemies in the Middle East.

Saddam Hussein was the one who got away.

As much as Hussein had a big target painted on his head, he was a difficult nut to crack. He had a loyal cadre of followers and a few body doubles, so assassinating or capturing him proved to be difficult.

So, some of the bright minds in the CIA decided that the blackmail porn thing they'd thought of 40 years earlier was a good idea. As with the Sukarno film, the script was for Hussein to appear to have been caught having sex on a secretly taped video or film. It would appear jerky and grainy to give it authenticity.

118

But the most important part was with who the Saddam look-alike would be starring. It couldn't be a Western sex worker or one of Hussein's allies' wives: it would have to be a man.

The CIA reasoned that the Islamic views toward homosexuality would go a long way to help discredit the dictator. They hoped to make the film lurid enough that when they distributed it to their assets around Iraq, it would soon make Hussein either a laughing stock, despised, or both.

Eventually, though, the heads of the Agency put an end to the mission.

But the CIA ended up winning with another one of its crazy missions - "proving" that Hussein had a stockpile of weapons of mass destruction. As you probably know, the CIA's "intel" on that led to the American-led 2003 invasion of Iraq.

Although the production on the "Hussein Film" may have ended, the CIA wasn't done with their pornography production in the Middle East. According to some former CIA officers, as the hunt for Osama bin Laden intensified in the early 2000s, the Agency produced a bizarre video to discredit the terrorist leader.

The video depicts CIA officers who look Middle Eastern, dressed like the Taliban and sitting around a campfire, drinking booze, and joking about having sex with boys. One of the men is a dead ringer for bin Laden, suggesting that the leader enjoyed engaging in activities that were clearly *haram* to any fundamentalist Muslim.

Although the movie was filmed, it was later determined to be too cheesy, even for the CIA thus ending, at least for the time being, the intelligence agency's foray into the porn business.

THE GONG SHOW AND THE CIA

The 1970s was the golden age of game shows on American television. The daytime airwaves were filled with shows like *The Dating Game*, *The Newlywed Game*, and of course, *The Gong Show*. Besides all being big hits in the '70s, all three of these game shows were produced by Chuck Barris.

Barris was '*the*' game show producer in the 1970s and was in demand for his production services by the TV networks well into the 1980s. But after a string of failures, Barris temporarily left TV land in 1984 and wrote a shocking memoir titled *Confessions of a Dangerous Mind*.

The book wasn't shocking because of any lurid tales it talked about Hollywood orgies or abuse and corruption behind the screen. Instead, it gained notoriety for the claims Barris made about his other job.

Barris made the bold claim that during the 1960s and '70s, while he was producing and even starring in game shows, he had also served as a CIA assassin.

Say what?

These claims have been vociferously denied by CIA representatives, yet they were interesting enough to be made into a film of the same name in 2002, starring Sam Rockwell as

Barris. The movie focused on Barris' hitman claims from his book, detailing how he killed his 33 victims with a variety of methods and in serval different circumstances, some of which are quite humorous.

So, it's just a movie, right? There's no way that the unassuming-looking Barris – a really below-average looking guy - could've been a killer for the CIA. Why would the CIA hire Barris in the first place?

Well, not everyone is convinced that all Barris claimed was a lie. And if his tales are even partially true, it would mean the missions he did with the CIA were among the craziest and certainly deserving of being included in this list. So, let's take a deeper look at the possibility of Chuck Barris being a top CIA assassin.

From TV Producer to Assassin?

To answer this question, we first must determine if it is at all possible, and to do that, we have to begin with the CIA.

Is it possible the CIA hired or subcontracted a game show producer to do assassinations?

If you've read this book from the start to this point, then I'm sure you'll agree that the answer is yes. We've seen how the CIA has used paramilitaries to kill their enemies during the Vietnam War and how they attempted to assassinate Castro on several occasions.

And these are just some of the cases they've admitted to. You can be sure that there have been countless other assassinations carried out by CIA officers, agents, subcontractors, or cutouts around the world.

Although the CIA has generally preferred to blackmail or turn its targets in other ways, murder was/is certainly a method they were/are willing to use if need be.

But would the CIA use a TV producer with no background in law enforcement, the military, intelligence, or any form of espionage?

Also based on what you've read so far, I'm sure you'll also agree the answer to this is yes.

We've seen how the CIA manipulated the American media through numerous well-placed assets in Operation Mockingbird. Considering how the CIA also had influence in Hollywood beginning in the 1950s and how that influence has continued into the present, it should be no surprise that the Agency has plenty of assets in Tinseltown that it uses in a variety of different ways.

John Chambers is the perfect example of a Hollywood insider who transitioned to being a CIA officer, even working in both fields simultaneously for a time. Although Chambers was no assassin, at least not that we're aware of, he personally demonstrates the CIA-Hollywood connection and how the CIA was always looking for people with unique talents.

So. if the CIA wasn't above assassinating people and if it utilized people from Hollywood, then there is a possibility Chuck Barris could've been an assassin.

But is there anything about Barris' background that would point toward him being a professional killer?

Chuck Barris was born to a Jewish family in Philadelphia, Pennsylvania in 1929. Contrary to the film's portrayal of Barris' early life, which depicted his mother dressing him in girl's clothing and his father as a serial killer, there was nothing really special or interesting about his early years. His father was perfectly sane and by all account was a legal dentist, and his mother was a typical housewife of the era.

Barris was a little too young to serve in World War II and when the Korean War broke out, he was attending Drexel University in Philadelphia. Barris majored in journalism and wrote for the student paper, *The Triangle*. Normally this wouldn't be a big deal, but if you remember, the CIA began influencing student newspapers in Operation Mockingbird during the 1950s.

Did a young Chuck Barris become involved with the CIA before he graduated from Drexel in 1953?

After graduating, Barris immediately found work in television and worked as a music producer and songwriter as well. He was then promoted to the head of daytime TV programming with the ABC network in the early 1960s, while in his thirties. It was quite the position for a young man and one that few people his age, and without apparent connections in the industry, could hope to land.

It was almost as if there was an unseen force, or forces, helping to propel Barris' career.

Well, that and a faked resume that got his foot in the door as a page at NBC.

Barris' first big TV hit was *The Dating Game*, which began airing in 1965. That was also about the time Barris claims he did his first hit for the CIA.

As outlandish as Barris' claims may seem at first, he does do a good job of logically explaining how something so seemingly

123

impossible was possible. Barris wrote that he was never an *official* CIA officer - in fact, he claimed later in his life that he once applied for the CIA but was rejected - but was a subcontractor or a "cut out" who was hired to give the Agency plausible deniability.

According to his memoir, Barris answered a want ad for the CIA but due to his amoral personality, they decided to train him as a killer, sending him to a secret training camp where he learned all the tools and techniques of murder. Then they gave him a CIA handler.

Barris even claims the CIA gave him some ideas for *The Dating Game*, including offering the winning couple trips to exotic locales where they were accompanied by a "chaperone." Barris wrote that he sometimes went with the couples to commit assassinations.

It all seems pretty unbelievable and something a Hollywood producer would come up with as a way to revive his lagging career, which it temporarily did for Barris in the mid-1980s.

After *Confessions* was released in 1984, Barris did the routine rounds on talk shows to promote the book and even told interviewers on *The Today Show* that he made up all the crazy claims. Case solved, the story is over, right?

Not quite.

Despite stating in 1984 that it was all a big hoax, Barris claimed in later years that *most* of his memoir was true. And as strange as it all sounded, people who knew him personally didn't discount the accusations out of hand. They pointed out that Barris regularly took impromptu trips and that he always seemed to be hiding something.

"There could be truth in the book because Chuck was so politically active. That's not to say I'd like to think Chuck killed all those innocent people," Barris' film producer friend, Andrew Lazar, said. "I think the book was not 100 percent true. I think there were strong grains of truth in the book."

So, if anything in *Confessions* was true, why would Barris write about it? It seems counterproductive to write all that down and bring on the wrath of the CIA, or other organizations, right? Well, he implies that the reason he wrote the book was to protect himself: the CIA wouldn't have a guy murdered who'd just written a tell-all book, he reasoned.

This brings it all back to Barris.

Is it possible that a fast-talking, below-average looking, and not so athletic guy with no military or law enforcement background could've done work for the CIA? The answer is obviously yes. We've seen how the CIA had its tentacles (and still probably does) in film, entertainment, and the media, so it's quite believable that Chuck Barris was an asset at some time for them.

But a professional assassin?

It may be crazy to consider, but this book is all about the most outlandish missions, projects, and things the CIA has done, and if there's one thing, we've learned so far, it's that the CIA apparently never considered anything too crazy to try.

Maybe the CIA really did use a goofy-looking TV producer as an assassin!

DID YOU KNOW?

- list actor and director George Clooney is another Hollywood insider with CIA connections. Clooney directed and starred in *Confessions of a Dangerous Mind* and *The Men Who Stare at Goats*, produced *Argo*, and starred in the CIA black comedy *Burn After Reading* and the action epic *Syriana*. Clooney had to research the CIA extensively for his roles by hanging out with current and former officers.

- After Jim Channon was done with his military service, he became a consultant for corporations where he transformed his hippy warrior monk vision from the battlefield into the boardroom. In a 2004 interview with the author of *The Men Who Stare at Goats*, Channon claimed the First Earth Battalion was still in existence, but neither the Army nor the CIA would confirm or deny it.

- A 1965 military coup in Indonesia left President Sukarno as a figurehead. The military, allied with Islamists, and likely with CIA support, took complete power by placing Sukarno in house arrest in 1967. Sukarno's health rapidly declined and he died of kidney failure in 1970 at the age of 69.

- The recent protests and riots in Hong Kong have not yet been classified as a Color Revolution, partially because the protesters were not a unified movement, with their demands varying widely. With that said, the Chinese government, as well as numerous reporters, have accused the CIA of playing a role in the unrest.

- The CIA's interest in removing Sukarno from power was quite pronounced, although not as intense as it was toward Castro. Before he was fighting communists and helping drug runners in the Golden Triangle, CIA operative Anthony Poshepny led a CIA operation to start an insurgency against Sukarno in the jungles of Indonesia. Although Poshepny wasn't successful, the CIA was impressed with his abilities, so they gave him the gig in the Golden Triangle.

NO ONE REALLY CARES
ABOUT GUATEMALA

Of course, that isn't quite true. The more than 17 million people who call Guatemala their home care about their country. And, of course, there are millions of other people around the world who have interests in the tiny yet densely populated Central American country. But the reality is that Guatemala is one of those countries that most people would have a hard time locating on a map.

What Guatemala has been known for, though, is its production of a lot of bananas, coffee, and sugar, which created a lot of interest among American-based corporations in the years after World War II.

The Soviet Union was also interested in Guatemala in those years, supporting the country's communist party, usually behind the scenes.

So, therefore, since the Soviet Union had an interest in Guatemala in the 1950s, and since Guatemala is close to the United States, the CIA developed a deep interest in the Latin American country.

And when you mix communism, corporate interests, and the CIA in a country that most people know little about, you get one of the most brazen CIA missions of all.

Today, the CIA is known for its many attempts to overthrow governments and to otherwise influence the course of politics and elections in foreign countries. Many of these later missions were based on the CIA 1954 mission, Operation PBSuccess, which was an intricate plot that overthrew the democratically-elected Guatemalan President Jacobo Arbenez Guzman.

Operation PBSuccess ripped the mask off the CIA, showing the world all of the ridiculous steps, the intelligence agency was willing to take to carry out its mission.

The Fruits of Communism

Guatemala is a country that has traditionally been overlooked. After attaining its independence from Spain in 1821, it went through years of growing pains, with most of the other current Central American nations also breaking away and forming their own governments. By the late 1800s, most people didn't know where Guatemala was or what it was known for, except for American fruit companies.

In 1899, the United Fruit Company (UFC) formed, quickly becoming the top fruit company in the world; it's still at the top of the industry, as Chiquita Brands International. As the entire world was ignoring Guatemala, the UFC saw its true potential.

The UFC came to Guatemala for its bananas and stayed for the power it was able to hold over the tiny country. The UFC's interest in Guatemala at first looked like a win for the company and a win for the country, as the company invested in railroads and other critical infrastructure.

But before too long, it became clear that the UFC was only interested in Guatemala's infrastructure to get more of its product to the country's only port, which the UFC happened to own.

The UFC eventually became a shadow government within Guatemala, doing whatever it wanted, or having the police and military under President Jorge Ubico do its bidding. The UFC cracked down on labor protests and owned all the good land in Guatemala.

Needless to say, many Guatemalans were not happy with the situation.

And here is where a combination of corruption and greed became intertwined with communism to create this strange situation.

The Guatemalan people revolted in 1944 and elected Juan Jose Arevalo in 1945. Arevalo was a true reformer and a moderate for the most part. He limited some of the UFC's power but didn't go so far as to initiate land reform.

Still, the Soviets had their agents in the country and the far-left parties were gaining ground, which was unwelcome news for American President Henry Truman.

Truman authorized the CIA Operation PBFortune in 1951 when leftist candidate Jacobo Arbenz was elected president. The operation, which was the most ambitious in the life of the new intelligence agency, called for a coup to overthrow Arbenz. But it was perhaps not ambitious enough for the time.

The CIA would have to wait for its next chance in 1953 under President Eisenhower.

A Phony War

When CIA director Allen Dulles brought the plans for Operation PBSuccess to President Eisenhower, he knew he had an ally in the Whitehouse. Eisenhower was ready and willing to fight communism anywhere in the globe, with any tools, which was music to the ears of Dulles.

Dulles may truly have been an ardent anti-communist, but he and his brother, Secretary of State John Dulles, were also shareholders in the UFC, so he also had a financial incentive to topple Arbenz.

Especially after Decree 900 passed on June 17, 1952.

Decree 900 wasn't really that radical. It didn't nationalize the UFC and it didn't hamper their ability to do business in Guatemala, but it did redistribute uncultivated land that it owned to the peasants.

This wasn't going to fly with the UFC, so the company called in favors it had with Dulles and the CIA to put the coup into action.

The CIA needed to have a Guatemalan face for their coup, so they appointed army officer Carlos Castillo Armas to lead the charge. Armas wasn't the most popular guy in Guatemala or within the Army, but he also wasn't necessarily unpopular. The problem was that Arbenz and Decree 900 *were* popular, so creating a grassroots base of support for Armas was nearly impossible.

He could only manage to round up about 500 men.

The CIA had its hands full trying to overthrow the Guatemalan government, but the "invasion" of Guatemala began on June 15, 1954, when Armas led four teams of his men into the nation from the neighboring countries of Honduras and El Salvador.

And here is where the CIA's propensity to think outside the box paid off.

So far, most of this reads like a standard operation to overthrow a government, with nothing too crazy happening, right? The real crazy part of this mission began as Armas and his force were working their way through the jungles and mountains of Guatemala, taking casualties along the way. If things kept up as they'd started, there was a good chance Armas wouldn't have any men left when he reached Guatemala City.

But the CIA really only needed him and a couple of other guys to march into the presidential palace.

As Armas and his band of right-wing revolutionaries were plodding through the jungles, the CIA was conducting its greatest campaign of propaganda and disinformation to that point in its history.

Guatemalan radio stations and newspapers reported hundreds of government soldiers wounded, refugees fleeing for Mexico, and Armas' troops winning battle after battle. A June 26 radio broadcast said two columns of Armas' anti-communist "Liberation Army" was about 50 miles from the capital and would certainly be there within days.

In response, the government declared martial law and ordered everyone to stay inside their homes.

The police chief of Guatemala City then made this startling address on the radio:

"To all Department Governors in the Republic. Capture immediately all mayors and other anti-Communist city officials currently affiliated with parties of the revolution."

The radio broadcasters then implored the Guatemalan people to join the Liberation Army because Arbenz would never surrender peacefully.

The truth is, though, that almost none of what was said on the radio broadcasts was true.

Safe in a small radio station in Miami, Florida, CIA officers and assets fluent in Spanish began broadcasting as the pirate station "Voice of Liberation" when the CIA coup began, claiming they were broadcasting live from the jungles in Guatemala.

The plan was immediately successful.

Other media outlets began reporting Voice of Liberation's broadcasts as factual, which caused the unions and other supporters of Arbenz to stay home and not protest in the streets. Most importantly, it demoralized the government troops and police who decided that they too would stay home and watch the events from a distance.

The reality is that Armas and his men lost several battles, but as they slogged their way closer to the capital, more and more demoralized government soldiers came over to their side.

Arbenz resigned from the presidency on June 27, 1954. He was allowed to leave peacefully to live his life in exile, never to return to his home country.

It was believed that the CIA had an assassination list but that everyone on the list was allowed to leave the country as exiles. Why would the CIA bother killing anyone at that point? Their crazy little plan had worked, Armas was put into power, and everything was back to normal.

Well, not exactly.

Armas was assassinated in 1957 by a leftist and Guatemala descended into more than 30 years of civil war. But that's nothing to the CIA. After all, war is good for business, and during the Cold War, business was fine.

Operation PBSuccess was also a good dry run for some of the CIA's later crazy missions. We've seen how the CIA has manipulated the media, used various forms of psychological warfare, and attempted - sometimes successfully - to overthrow numerous governments.

It all began with a little country that few people knew, or cared about at the time, with a truly ludicrous mission called Operation PBSuccess.

EXPORTING CIA VIOLENCE
SOUTH OF THE BORDER

What do you get when you mix the violence and terror of the Phoenix Program with the Latin flavor of Project PBSuccess? Operation Condor, of course!

Named for the largest bird of prey in the world, the Andean condor, Operation Condor was a cooperative, transnational intelligence and paramilitary operation carried out by the leaders of the right-wing dictatorships in the Southern Cone nations of South America - Argentina, Chile, Uruguay, Brazil, Bolivia, and Paraguay - in the 1970s. At first, it was against communist guerilla groups but eventually shifted to be against any of their political enemies.

Operation Condor became known for its extreme acts of violence that were as unique as they were brutal: soccer stadiums became prisons, people routinely "disappeared," and planes and helicopters were used to give enemies of the state one-way flights into oblivion.

This intense operation was carried out by the intelligence agencies and militaries of the Southern Cone nations, but behind this campaign were the ever-watchful eyes of the CIA. In recent years, the CIA has admitted to providing logistical support and communications equipment to the member nations and has also confessed to having knowledge of some of the more brutal aspects of Operation Condor.

But as information about this intense operation began to be revealed to the public in the 2000s, it became clear that many in the CIA, if not the Agency itself, had played an active role at times. Some of the "interrogation" methods used by Operation Condor operatives were eerily similar to those used by the CIA in the Phoenix Program and CIA agents were plentiful, and often living in the open, in South America during the 1970s.

The CIA had also learned from Operation PBSuccess how to use psychology and psychological warfare to gain an edge in very unconventional warfare, often referred to as the "Guerra Sucia," or "Dirty War," in Argentina.

By the time Operation Condor was over in the late 1980s, thousands were dead and hundreds to thousands more were "missing" and presumed dead. Operation Condor was the most expansive and brutal combined intelligence-military operation in the Western Hemisphere, which has people from many countries demanding to know just how deeply the CIA was involved.

Fighting the Red Scourge

To understand how bizarre Operation Condor was and how crazy it was for the CIA to be involved, we have to set the scene. The leaders of the nations of the Southern Cone officially formed the alliance in 1975 to fight the communist/Marxist threat in South America.

Remember, this was the Cold War. The USSR and USA never went to war directly against each other, but they used the rest of the world as their proxies to try to advance their influence and systems of government.

The Soviets thought that Latin America was ripe for the picking.

Most Latin American countries were poor, had corrupt pro-capitalist governments, and had mixed feelings toward the United States. The Soviets thought that Castro and Cuba embodied this general feeling, so they hoped to use Cuba as a beachhead to promote their ideas and hopefully turn more countries in the region to communism.

But as much as the Soviets claimed they wanted to be the saviors of the poor and oppressed masses of Latin America, they really didn't understand the region or the people.

Not all men in Latin America were smoking cigars and wearing goatee beards, and not all Latin Americans wanted to overthrow their governments.

Overall, the culture of Latin America was, and still is, more socially conservative and heavily influenced by the Roman Catholic Church. Most people don't buy Marx's whole "religion is the opiate of the masses" bit.

And the countries of Latin America are diverse from country to country.

Compared to the rest of Latin America, the Southern Cone nations tend to be larger in physical size and population, wealthier, more educated, and generally have a higher standard of living. The people of the Southern Cone also tend to be more ethnically European, largely as the result of massive immigration from Spain, Italy, Portugal, Ireland, Germany, and Russia to Argentina, Uruguay, Chile, and southern Brazil.

In fairness to the Soviets/Russians, the Americans didn't really understand Latin America too well either. They tended to project American ideas of capitalism versus socialism, which were very black and white during the Cold War, onto Latin Americans, who were inclined to see the differences more in degrees.

All these differences in philosophies and perceptions came to a head in the early 1970s, when violent leftist guerilla groups, such as the Tupamaros and the Monteneros, were committing kidnappings, assassinations, and bombings in the name of communist revolution throughout the Southern Cone.

The KGB and CIA were at times openly involved in the situation, which reached a crisis point in 1973.

In 1970, the people of Chile democratically elected socialist Salvador Allende as president. Allende wasn't very radical and his election didn't raise too many eyebrows in the United States at first, but when he started nationalizing American companies, things changed quickly.

Apparently, Allende thought he'd do his own version of Decree 900.

After the success of Operation PBSuccess, there was no way the CIA was going to let another Latin American leader cut into US profits. The thing was, though, that Chile was much farther from the US than Guatemala, and it was considerably larger in population. The cheesy but effective psychological games they'd played in Guatemala probably wouldn't work on the

Chilean people, so they found an inside guy who was much more capable than Carlos Armas.

The CIA appealed to Chilean Army General Augusto Pinochet's patriotism, hatred of communism, and of course, his greed, to entice him to overthrow Allende. The CIA agreed to provide Pinochet with intelligence and logistical support, letting him know what officers he could trust and the best time and place to make a move on Allende.

The coup happened quickly, with Allende being overthrown and killed on September 11, 1973.

After Pinochet took power, the CIA was giddy with its victory. It looked around the Southern Cone and saw plenty of opportunities to play its cloak and dagger games and possibly to initiate some of its crazier ideas. Paraguay, Brazil, and Bolivia had already been ruled by dictators for years, Uruguay joined their ranks in June 1973, and Argentina was ripe for change.

The CIA had plenty of resources and ideas, and the Southern Cone was the perfect place to carry them out.

Not an Airplane Ride You'd Want to Take

Once Operation Condor got underway, the DINA (Chilean intelligence) and SIDA (Argentine intelligence), as well as all the participating intelligence, military, and paramilitary groups had to devise a way to communicate with each other safely and quickly.

This is where the CIA became involved.

In a time before the internet, intelligence agencies had to use encryption devices to send top-secret messages. This was state-of-the-art technology at the time and because of that, there were only a few companies in the world that made the devices.

Like the Swiss company Crypto AG.

But the truth is, Crypto AG was just another CIA front company.

Crypto AG was started in 1952 by Russian Swede cryptologist Boris Hagelin and shortly thereafter, the CIA became its main investor. In the early 1970s, the West German intelligence agency, BND, invested in the company, after which the CIA and BND created Operation Rubikon.

Operation Rubikon is an outrageous little postscript to Operation Condor and could be a separate chapter in this book. According to recently released documents, more than 120 countries were customers of Crypto AG from the 1950s through the 2000s, which means that the CIA and BND likely spied on all of them. Some of those countries were behind the Iron Curtain, but more than a few, such as Italy and Greece, were NATO allies.

The CIA admits they read quite a few messages between Operation Condor agencies, and they were quite lurid.

There was regular talk of kidnappings, torture, and assassinations. The various militaries and intelligence agencies worked together, sending suspected radicals across national boundaries to be tortured for more information. Often the suspects ended up in Argentina where they were tortured in a variety of ways and then loaded into a plane or helicopter and pushed out over the Rio de la Plata River or the Atlantic Ocean.

The DINA and Chilean military also took prisoners on these "night flights" over the Pacific Ocean where they were thrown into a watery grave from thousands of feet.

The CIA certainly knew these things were going on, but today they claim they didn't participate in any of these activities.

But how true is that?

CIA officers were operating throughout the Southern Cone during the Cold War, sometimes quite openly. CIA officers and assets played a critical role in the overthrow of Allende and most of them likely stayed in place in the aftermath.

But in fairness to the CIA, they did stop at least one assassination.

A CIA officer stationed in Uruguay in 1976 was spending some time at a local bar when he heard some known Operation Condor operatives talking about assassinating an American politician. It isn't clear if the CIA officer was conducting surveillance or if he was participating in an operation with the Condor agents - or both - but he was a bit surprised to hear them talking about killing US Congressman Ed Koch.

Yes, the same Ed Koch who was later mayor of New York City and after that went on to star on the reality show *The People's Court*. He pushed hard to cut off funding to the Uruguayan government for its human rights abuses.

The potential assassination was averted when the State Department persuaded the Uruguayan government to keep the alleged ringleaders in South America, far from Koch.

The CIA's complicated and twisted web in South America was further complicated by its involvement in the School of the Americas.

The School of the Americas may sound like it was some type of boarding school, but it was really a place where Latin American

141

military and intelligence officers learned their crafts from American experts. Located at the Fort Benning Army base in Columbus, Georgia, Latin American officers got crash courses in everything from communications to counter-insurgency operations. One of the training manuals used at the camp emphasized many of the tactics the CIA used in the Phoenix Program during the Vietnam War.

Many of those tactics, such as rape as a torture weapon and attacking family members of targets when targets couldn't be located, were used in Operation Condor. And there were some pretty notable School of the Americas alumni who went on to play major roles in Operation Condor.

Argentine dictator General Jorge Videla was one of the most prominent graduates, but along with him were Bolivian President Hugo Suarez and Chilean DINA head Manuel Contreras, all of whom played major roles in Operation Condor.

Ultimately, Operation Condor proved to be one of the biggest black spots on the CIA's record, which obviously included several black spots. As much as the Agency has attempted to mitigate its participation in the operation, there's no denying its officers played a major role. The CIA provided the communication equipment Condor agents used to carry out their deeds.

The CIA, along with the Army, also trained many of the major players in Operation Condor, who then brought their "skills" to the Southern Cone. And although we don't know for sure if CIA officers were actively torturing and killing enemies of the Southern Cone governments, it's not too crazy to think they were.

In fact, the more that's revealed about Operation Condor and the CIA, the more it seems like nothing is too crazy to believe.

THE DRUG SMUGGLING CIA?
PART TWO

Keeping things south of the border, let's take a look at another accusation of CIA drug running.

It was the 1980s: new wave was the cool music, big hair was the rage, and Americans just couldn't get enough cocaine. The cocaine that Americans of all classes and backgrounds - from Wall Street to Main Street and from the urban centers to the suburbs and even rural areas - was getting high on obviously came from somewhere outside the United States. Cocaine is a processed drug that is derived from the coca plant, which is native to the rainforests of South America.

Peru and Bolivia were the first major cocaine-producing countries, followed by Columbia in the 1970s. The Columbians brought cocaine production to a new level, as they organized cartels that were able to control and protect their crops, build labs to process the plants into drugs, bribe or threaten government officials, and smuggle the finished drugs out of the country.

The number one destination for South American cocaine in the 1970s and '80s was the United States but getting there presented some problems.

And this is where this collection of CIA "missions" gets truly crazy.

When the communist Sandinista Party came to power in Nicaragua through a 1979 revolution, it immediately changed Cold War dynamics in the Western Hemisphere. The US government was suddenly faced with a new communist country, albeit a small one, in its backyard. American military and intelligence leaders began scrambling to figure out what happened and how things could be constrained or reversed.

It was clear the CIA had "dropped the ball."

But with that said, there were plenty of opportunities for the CIA to right the ship. US support for the right-wing Nicaraguan guerillas known as the Contras allowed the CIA to fight the Sandinistas. The problem for the CIA was this pesky little thing called the Constitution.

In 1982, the US Congress passed the Boland Amendment, which outlawed US funding of the Contras to openly overthrow the Sandinista government. There were gray areas of the amendment, and no organization understands gray areas like the CIA.

By the late 1980s, rumors and reports began being published that the CIA was allowing the Contras to smuggle cocaine through Central America to the United States to help fund their insurgency against the Sandinistas. The allegations alleged many American drug smugglers worked with the Contras, as well as Columbians, to flood the US with cocaine.

The CIA has denied allegations that it took part in drug smuggling from Latin America, but as the saying goes, "where there's smoke" - which in this case is coming from a crack or freebase pipe - "then there's fire."

144

Funding the Revolution

The CIA's potential involvement in Central American drug smuggling may seem straightforward at first, but it's actually very convoluted. Besides allegations of the Contras smuggling dope, their enemies the Sandinistas also took part in smuggling and the Columbian cartels were there to profit from both sides.

So, before we get to all that, let's start with Nicaragua.

Located just a couple of countries south of Guatemala is Nicaragua, and like Guatemala, Nicaragua has historically struggled with poverty and being overshadowed, and at times directly controlled, by other countries. First, it was the Spanish, then the Mexicans to a certain extent, and later the Americans.

Due to a combination of Nicaragua's poverty, the corrupt and oppressive nature of the Nicaraguan government, and the romantic allure of revolution (the first two reasons appealed to the majority of the people, while the third was the reason for idealistic middle and upper-class youth to join), the Sandinistas built a large, well-organized political party *and* army that came to power.

But as we mentioned earlier, if you're a tiny communist country in the Yankees' back yard, you're going to have some problems, no matter how much support you get from Cuba or the Soviet Union.

When Ronald Reagan became the American president in 1981, he made going after Nicaragua one of his top priorities, but he was hampered by the Boland Amendment. So, to work around the Amendment's stricter prohibitions, he had training camps built for the Contras in Honduras and Guatemala. The Contras were then trained by US Special Forces and the CIA.

The Contras just needed a supply of cash, or guns, or both to conduct their counterrevolution.

Contras, Cartels, and Cocaine Cowboys

The first reports that the CIA may be involved in an intricate drug smuggling scheme with the Contras and the cartels began surfacing in the mid-1980s. Government reports admitted that some Contras were smuggling cocaine to pay for their operations but that the CIA didn't have anything to do with it.

But how did the government know the Contras were smuggling dope in the first place?

These reports were followed by a US Senate investigation led by then-Senator John Kerry. Kerry's committee uncovered a bit more, including how the State Department, which essentially means "the CIA," paid over $800,000 to companies owned by Contra drug traffickers.

These allegations were quickly forgotten, although they quietly lingered until the 1990s when journalist Gary Webb wrote a series of articles titled "Dark Alliance" in *The San Jose Mercury News* in 1995.

Webb's new allegations were explosive, to say the least.

Webb interviewed hundreds of people in the US and Central America for his series and concluded that the smuggling operation was quite complex but involved three major players. The two primary smugglers were Oscar Blandon and Norwin Menses, who were Contras with known CIA connections.

Blandon was actually arrested for smuggling large amounts of cocaine into the US in 1992. It was enough dope for him to spend a better part of the rest of his life in prison, but instead, he cooperated with the DEA and got time served.

How convenient, huh?

One of the people he informed on was a San Francisco Bay area drug kingpin named Rick Ross.

Ross built his empire in the 1980s by buying cocaine from Blandon and Menses, turning the coke into crack and then selling the crack to Black gangs in Los Angeles. Ross was given a life sentence in 1996 but later had his sentence reduced and was released from prison in 2009.

Although Webb didn't have a smoking crack pipe/gun that could definitively prove the CIA was helping smuggle cocaine into the US, it certainly looked that way. Despite the revelations, Webb faced strong pushback against his series. Of course, the CIA and most of the government denied everything, but what was most curious is how *The New York Times* and *The Los Angeles Times* also jumped on board to deny Webb's allegations.

Then Gary Webb was discovered by his wife, dead in their suburban Sacramento, California apartment on December 10, 2004. The investigation found that he had died from two gunshot wounds to the head.

The coroner ruled Garry Webb's death a suicide!

Um, okay, I guess anything's possible...

Many believe Webb's research only uncovered the tip of the iceberg and the truth is that the CIA's involvement in this crazy scheme went much, much deeper.

Rick Ross wasn't the only American civilian to get involved in large-scale drug smuggling from Central America, possibly, or more than likely, under the watchful eyes of the CIA. Louisiana pilot Barry Seal's story also seems to implicate the CIA in some major smuggling operations.

Barry Seal's life was going great in the 1960s when he was a young and upwardly mobile pilot with TWA, but then he was busted trying to smuggle some explosives into Mexico. He was fired from his job but somehow avoided legal repercussions.

Seal avoided a lot of legal repercussions throughout his life. It was almost like he had an angel hovering over him. Angels may exist, but they aren't particularly known to favor drug runners, so to find out who was protecting Seal, keep reading.

After losing his job with TWA, Seal turned to drug smuggling, which landed him in a Mexican prison for a brief stay. As bad as those prisons are, Seal managed to make plenty of contacts with Central Americans and a notorious American smuggler named Roger Reaves.

Reaves hooked Seal up with Columbian contacts, including drug lord Pablo Escobar. With the contacts he had made in Central America, Barry Seal now had a drug pipeline that extended from Columbia to Mena, Arkansas.

Mena, Arkansas?

Yes, Seal kept his planes at a small airport in Mena, Arkansas, which Reaves also claimed was one of the points where plenty of cocaine was brought into the US under the CIA's purview and while future President Bill Clinton was governor of the state in the 1980s.

The CIA has admitted to a "two-week exercise" it conducted at Mena in the 1980s, although it has denied any drug smuggling.

But this crazy story only gets crazier.

Seal was arrested, tried, and convicted of drug smuggling in 1984, but avoided prison time by working with the DEA and CIA. His primary mission was to collect evidence on Escobar and his associates, which led him into Nicaragua that year.

It turns out the Contras weren't the only Nicaraguans smuggling dope into the US; the Sandinistas had a deal with Escobar to smuggle cocaine on Seal's planes.

The DEA later claimed that they intercepted the only load of dope that Seal smuggled in from Nicaragua, which may or may not be true. What is known, though, is that an American general gave a public speech mentioning how the Sandinistas were involved in drug smuggling to the US.

The speech effectively "burned" Seal as a CIA asset, although he continued to work for the DEA in the US until he was gunned down by Columbian hitmen in Baton Rouge in 1986.

All evidence indicates the killers were associated with Escobar and the Medellin Cartel, but there were probably few tears shed for him at the CIA as Seal was clearly a loose end.

Just like the allegations of CIA drug smuggling in the Golden Triangle, thanks to plausible deniability (there's that phrase is again!) the complete truth of the CIA's involvement in Central American drug smuggling will never be known. One thing is for sure though, as crazy as the situation in southeast Asia was, what took place with the Contras, Sandinistas, Columbians, cocaine Cowboys, and the CIA was even more bizarre.

IF YOU THINK THEY'RE WATCHING YOU, THEY PROBABLY ARE

The final entry in our book of ridiculous CIA missions is probably the craziest and perhaps most disturbing of all. It doesn't involve bizarre methods of torture, experiments in mind control, or the use of sex and drugs to get information. No, this final case involves the CIA's ongoing digital war on its enemies.

These missions don't involve guns, bombs, or poisons, but viruses, Trojan horses, and electronic devices. And despite the lack of traditional weapons, these CIA missions have inflicted just as much, if not more, collateral damage.

We're talking about the CIA's army of computer hackers.

That's right, since the early 2000s, the CIA has been at the forefront of the technology curve, employing more than 5,000 computer nerds who have written more than 1,000 malicious computer programs that can steal files, disrupt programs, and watch you from your TV even when it's off.

In this case, Big Brother truly is watching you!

The CIA's computer hacking missions are completed under the division known as the Center for Cyber Intelligence (CCI), which for the most part remained unknown until in March 2017 activist Julian Assange and the Wikileaks organization began releasing a series of documents known as Vault 7.

The documents elaborate on all the various programs, viruses, and other technologies the CIA has at its disposal, demonstrating that the Agency has access to the newest and craziest computer technology in the world.

As crazy as it may seem that the CIA has an army of hackers at its beckoning, what makes this whole case even crazier is that the CIA, the preeminent intelligence agency in the world - well, many would argue that honor goes to the KGB/FSB, and a few may say it's MI6 - "lost" much of this technology.

That's right, while CIA operatives were busy playing hacker, the electronic monstrosities they created were stolen and unleashed on the world.

Now that's pretty crazy!

First, They Had It, Then It Was Gone

The Vault 7 documents released by Wikileaks were immense and some would say quite damning toward the CIA. Well, that's if you ever heard about them. Although the Vault 7 documents were reported in the mainstream American media, they received minimal attention and almost no critical analysis. It was almost as if the major media outlets had a "nothing to see here" attitude toward Vault 7.

But there was plenty to see and read in the Vault 7 documents.

The Vault 7 documents included thousands of pages of top-secret CIA material relating to cybersecurity from 2013 through

2016. The documents were released periodically in 24 "dumps," beginning with "Year Zero" and ending with "Protego."

The document dumps revealed that the CIA can pretty much access any computer or electronic device it wants and that privacy is something that's an afterthought at best.

For instance, UMBRAGE is a collection of tools and techniques the CIA learned and stole from hackers around the world. Some of these tools include webcam capture, password collection, and data destruction.

In other words, UMBRAGE gives the CIA the ability to log into your computer, erase all your files, and then watch you on your webcam as you melt down after seeing what just happened.

It also gives the CIA the ability to place compromising files on a person's computer. If the CIA really wanted to "get rid" of someone without having to kill them, all they need to do is create a hidden file with criminal activity in it such as terrorism or child porn.

The CIA could then approach the target later and tell them to quit doing what they're doing or they'll go public with the file.

Assassination is so 20th century. Cyber blackmail is so much cleaner and more effective.

But wait, there's plenty more!

The CIA can track our movements via our smartphones, which we always carry, and capture data from our phones.

But the craziest of all the CIA cyber tools is called Weeping Angel.

Weeping Angel is the code name for a hacking tool that allows the CIA to monitor you through your smartTV. The program requires someone to install it on the TV with a USB stick but that only takes a few minutes—and an officer can be in and out without the target even knowing. Once the program is installed, the CIA can gain access to the TV's microphones and cameras.

Other documents released show that the CIA has been studying how to remotely control cars (the ones we drive, not toys) and internet routers.

All of this is pretty crazy, but the reality is most people weren't surprised when the Vault 7 documents were released. I mean, after all, this is the same organization that dosed random people with LSD, tortured people for information, overthrew foreign governments, and spied on their own allies, so the ethical bar wasn't set very high, to begin with, to put it mildly.

But what makes all this mass of crazy even crazier, and quite ironic, is how little security the CIA placed on all these tools/weapons.

It turns out that the CIA hackers pretty much lived in a world of their own and all but ignored the standard chain of command. The result was that "the CIA lost control of the majority of its hacking arsenal," as one Wikileaks document notes.

Well, I guess that's what happens when you have to hire civilian NEET hackers because all your people with intelligence and military experience are boomers who need help to turn on their computers.

So, in this case of having something and then losing it, what was the result?

Since the CIA will probably never reveal all, or even most of the facts, we can only guess. Since these cyber weapons are now loose, pretty much anyone with minimal computer knowledge can attain and use them. Terrorists, organized crime groups, and hostile state actors all now have access to these hacking tools.

It's just the sort of thing that instills plenty of confidence in the CIA of the future, right?

CONCLUSION

Wow! How was that for a ride through 21 of the most amazing CIA missions of all time? Some of these missions the CIA did were crazy in a brutal sort of way, like the Phoenix Program and Operation Condor, while others were just plain crazy.

Who in their right mind would think dosing random people with LSD was a good idea?

Or better yet, what were the CIA officers *really thinking* when they came up with the idea to use sex dolls as decoys?

If there are a few things that we can take away from this odyssey through cloak and dagger, it's that over the CIA's not so long history, relatively speaking, it has demonstrated the ability to think outside the box. Sometimes that unconventional thinking resulted in some brutal missions, while other times it led to some brutally funny operations.

In fact, the CIA was so far outside the box at times that as laughable as a game show host being a CIA contracted assassin may be, the more you think about all the crazy things the Agency has done, it's not so unbelievable after all, is it?

And as we move forward into the 2020s, there will undoubtedly be more crazy revelations revealed about the CIA. As the CIA and all the other "deep state" alphabet agencies gain more power through some of the surveillance equipment and techniques we profiled in the last chapter, they'll continue to push the envelope.

So, be vigilant and be careful — or *you* may become a victim of the CIA's next crazy mission!

MORE BOOKS BY BILL O'NEILL

 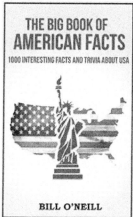 

I hope you enjoyed this book and
learned something new.

Please feel free to check out some
of my previous books on Amazon.

Printed in Great Britain
by Amazon